Pens & Pencil

A Collector's Handbook

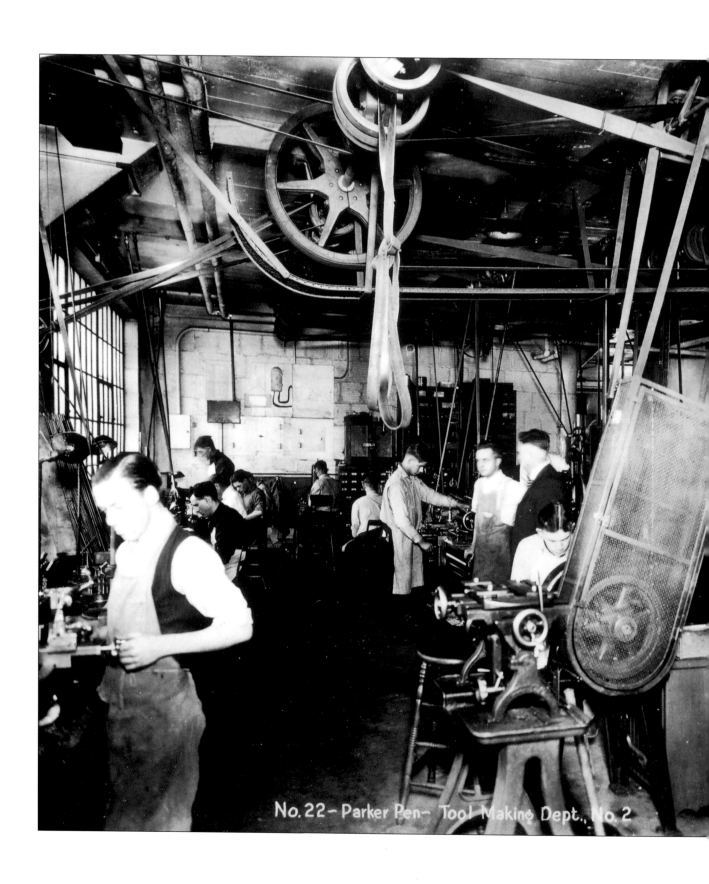

No. 22 - Parker Pen - Tool Making Dept., No. 2

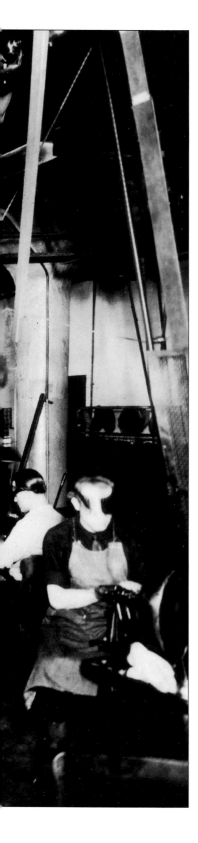

Pens & Pencils
A Collector's Handbook

Regina Martini
Photographed by Harald Grotowsky

4880 Lower Valley Road, Atglen, PA 19310 USA

The author thanks the following persons for their support:
Frau Hammad (Faber-Castel), Frau Heuer (Lamy), Frau Duchna-Voyatzis (Montblanc),
Frau Nagel (Parker), Frau Führmann (Pelikan), Frau Gorke (Rotring), Fray Grübel (Sheaffer)
Herr Zimmerlin (Waterman), and her husband Renato for his patience.

Library of Congress Cataloging-in-Publication Data

Martini, Regina.
Pens & pencils : a collector's handbook / by Regina Martini ;
photographed by Harald Grotowsky.
p. cm
Translated from the German.
ISBN 0-7643-0313-9 (paper)
1. Fountain pens -- Collectors and collecting. 2. Fountain pens-
-Catalogs. I. Title.
TS1266.M37 1996
681'.6--dc20   95-53836
CIP

Revised price guide 1998

Translated by Dr. Edward Force,
Central Connecticut State University

Photos: Harald Grotowsky, Pelikan Archives, Montblanc Archives
(Foto Medici, photo of Oscar Wilde)
All photos in the catalog section are of the Martini collection.

Printed in China
ISBN 0-7643-0313-9

Published by Schiffer Publishing Ltd.
4880 Lower Valley Road
Atglen, PA 19310
Phone: (610) 593-1777 Fax: (610) 593-2002
E-mail: Schifferbk@aol.com
Please write for Free catalog.
This book may be purchased from the publisher.
Please include $3.95 for shipping.
Try your bookstore first.

Contents

Introduction

What inspires so many people to collect certain things? From the beginning of time, there has been a primary human instinct to acquire things, have trading materials, and create values.

Everything that one can imagine is being collected. The best-known subjects for collecting are probably stamps and coins, jewelry (especially wristwatches), etc., etc. But everyday items are also chosen for collecting. Thus there are also fans of beer coasters, matchbooks, cigarette lighters...to name only a few.

For some years, the popularity of the fountain pen has been growing steadily. Though there were only a few serious collectors of these historically interesting objects in the early eighties, the number of writing-implement and fountain pen collectors has multiplied many times.

What is it that creates the popularity of the fountain pen? What inspires the fascination of collecting them? Is it simply just a desire for nostalgia? Is it a striving to complete certain areas? Or is it a kind of time travel, back to the good old days? The fact is, handwritten material is gaining greater significance today in the age of computer technology. Not only what is written, but how it is written, matters.

The fountain pen: What kind of history is hidden behind it? How many love letters may it have written? Under what conditions did it change owners? If only it could talk...

And now thousands of them lie in permanent collections and are treated with respect and love, just as they deserve!

Aspects of Collecting

Fountain pens can be collected in different ways. Since there are thousands of writing implements, many collectors concentrate on certain brands. This could be, for example, Parker, but handling this brand's full palette of products from 1888 to the present would exceed the boundaries of a single book. In parts of the twenties, this firm had up to 400 models on the market!

Along with Parker, the best-known firms are Montblanc, Pelikan, Waterman and Sheaffer. There is scarcely a collector who does not collect at least a few products of one of these manufacturers. But even assembling the various writing instruments made by one firm can be so vast and expensive and time-consuming that it could fill an entire lifetime.

Other collectors look only for pens from a certain country. Whoever collects German fountain pens will look for products of such firms as Montblanc, Pelikan, Kaweco, Soennecken, Osmia, Faber Castell, Geha, Lamy, Rotring, etc.

Collectors' items from America come, for the most part, from firms such as Waterman, Parker, Wahl-Eversharp, Sheaffer, Conklin, etc.

The collector of British fountain pens will look for Parker, Conway Stewart, Swan, Waterman, Onoto, etc.

Collectors of Italian writing implements will seek pens by Omas, Aurora, etc. Outside Italy, though, these pens are not very well known.

Collectors of French writing implements will look for pens by Waterman, Edacoto, Bayard, etc.

So when one begins to collect, one should think carefully about what guidelines one would like to follow. Probably every beginner will start by taking whatever he finds into his collection, in order to specialize later, when he knows what the individual manufacturers produced at what times.

Another possibility for specialization is the collection of fountain pens from specific decades. The pens of the twenties and thirties are surely among the most colorful and interesting. But pens from the forties are also very interesting in terms of design and color.

The manufacturers have always produced different models for different countries. This is because of the different factories involved, but also because of the differing tastes/preferences.

Thus there are, for example, different Waterman fountain pens in different colors in France from those in Germany.

Parker numbered several pens for the Italian market and always enclosed a numbered certificate; this was not done on the German market. At this time in America, Cross makes a fountain pen with a gold filled steel point, while in Germany it is only available with a gold point (Townshend Collection).

So it is a good idea to look beyond one's own boundaries when looking for variations on the pens on one's own market.

This book covers the histories of only five manufacturers--those whose products are collected the most.

This book also offers a large pictorial section with descriptions and values, and leaves it to the reader to build up and develop his collection on whatever basis he chooses. The concentration on definite areas, time periods, or brands can then develop as the collection grows.

No matter how and what you collect, the most important factor is always the joy in the individual object.

Value and Price Criteria

Unfortunately, with the growing popularity of fountain pens, their prices have also increased drastically. While it was formerly possible to purchase an interesting specimen at a flea market for a few dollars, today one must usually reach deeper into one's wallet. Often many dealers do business, not really knowledgeable of what they are doing, which usually results from comparison with present-day models.

For example, here is a comparison of Montblanc products. Unlike today, this firm formerly sold low-priced pens, even school pens. But since their pricing policy and variety of models has changed, settling in the higher-price range, many dealers are inclined to overvalue the old pieces, which are often very simple. For these dealers, and above all for the well-meaning collector, the section of this book gives an idea of present-day prices.

The listed prices in the catalog section always refer to pieces in perfect condition; that means that the pen contains all its original parts and, though it surely could have been used, it shows no signs of wear. In such cases, 100% of the listed price applies. It is very difficult to find such pieces, since most fountain pens are not working, at least in the filling system.

About 50% of the listed price is realistic if the pen shows serious faults, for example, if the point is no longer the original one, the clip is missing, the ink feed is broken, the cap is cracked or the filler has been discolored by leaking ink.

About 20% of the value can be paid if the pen is only usable as a source of spare parts. For example, the complete cap may have been exchanged or the barrel may have burn-holes.

In the last case, one should consider whether it is practical to pay for a pen that is obviously only good for parts.

If you should find a pen, though, in its original box with the original price label on it, a price increase of as much as 50% above the catalog price might be justified.

The book that lies before you cannot claim to be a complete price guide. There simply are too many pens for that. Yet it can be of help to you in making a decision and tell you the actual value of your pen.

More and more, historical pens are being sold by regular specialty shops or other stores. Here the prices are naturally higher, because these shops have their own ways of calculating prices. But at least the customer receives a legal guarantee, and that is certainly worth somewhat more.

In this catalog, more than 1800 pens made by Parker, Swan, Montblanc, Pelikan, Waterman and Sheaffer are valued. Also considered are: Conway Stewart, Mentmore, Wearever, Wahl-Eversharp, etc. The price listings are based on the results of international auctions and on personal experience. Many pens are becoming harder to find, while others are surely in your collection already. At the same time, this book can be used as a reference work for the pens produced by these firms. Along with the historical pens, present-day models that can be presently bought in stores also are shown. These are marked as to collecting value with the letters LP, to indicate their usual retail price. This information does not at all reflect the collector's value; rather, everyone can decide for himself whether the pen is worth that much to him. No matter how you use this book, it will offer information about pens and their prices.

For firms whose products are shown in the price section, the beginning and ending production dates, insofar as they are known, are stated. The years listed for the models are the years in which they were introduced. The circa (ca.) marking means that it was not possible to obtain definite information, but the pen was sold around that time. All this information is accurate according to my knowledge at the time of writing. All models that are mentioned but not depicted have belonged to me or are known to me. Naturally, absolutely complete lists are impossible.

The Ink-Filling System

This heading is actually slightly misleading. For at the beginning of the story of the fountain pen, there was not only the problem of how to get the ink into the pen, but also how to keep the ink in the filled "holder" without dripping and leaking out. It needs to be released in the right quantities when writing.

The "ink-filling" system thus had a threefold mission:
1. Taking up the ink.
2. Holding it in the pen.
3. Releasing it out to the point in the right quantity when writing.

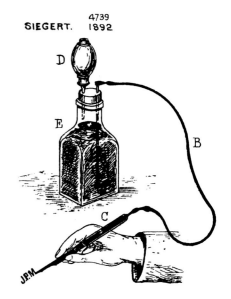

A suggestion made in 1892 by H. Siegert, to supply a "writer" with ink through a rubber tube. It did not fulfill one of the most important requirements, that of independence from the ink bottle.

In the pens that are collector's items today, these systems meet all the requirements listed above more or less perfectly.

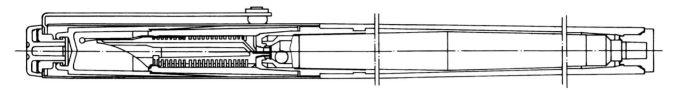

Jif-Waterman of France invented the ink cartridge...

...which is used by almost all manufacturers today. Here is a cross-section of a modern cartridge filler.

Cartridge: A plastic reservoir filled with ink and replaced after the ink is used up. Since the sixties, this has been the most commonly used and most convenient way of filling a fountain pen. Unfortunately, there is no all-inclusive standard. Many firms have their own norms.

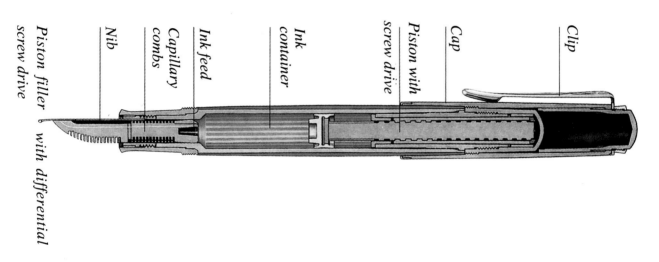

Piston filler--piston with screw drive

Piston: The ink is drawn in by using the piston on the rear part of the pen. The piston system has been used by Pelikan since 1929. Many other firms have adopted it. The pistons were formerly made of cork; now they are made of plastic.

Converter: A refillable cartridge. The ink tank is utilized instead of the cartridge. By means of the converter, bottle ink can be used. It can be added to the cartridge at any time.

The converter also exists with a turning mechanism (used, for example, by Waterman), or with a pulling mechanism (Parker) or a pressing mechanism (Sheaffer).

Lever Filler: On the side of the pen is a lever. Under it, a piece is attached that presses on an ink sac. One holds the pen point in the ink and lifts the lever all the way out, forming a right angle. This process is repeated three or four times; then the bladder is filled. This system was invented in the early 1900s and still marketed in the sixties. It was the usual filling system used by Sheaffer, Waterman, Swan, Wahl-Eversharp, Conway Stewart and others.

Button Filler: A cap is removed from the end of the barrel. Under it is a push button attached to a flexible piece of metal and an ink sac. By pressing down the button, ink is sucked in. This system was likewise popular in the twenties and was used by Parker, Montblanc and various British firms.

Safety Pen: The point is screwed outward for writing and screwed back in after being used. Filling with ink takes place when the point is inside the barrel. This system was used by Waterman, Montblanc, Soennecken and others.

Snorkel: By turning the plunger end of the barrel, a tube under the point is extended. This is placed in the ink. By moving the plunger up and down, the pen fills. Only Sheaffer used this system.

Capillary System: This system was used in the Parker "61"; a cartridge attached to the feed was placed in the ink and automatically pulled the ink in.

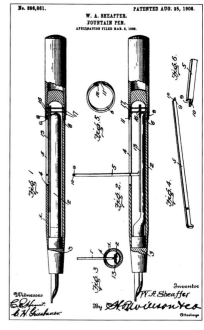

The patent of the Sheaffer firm for a lever filler.

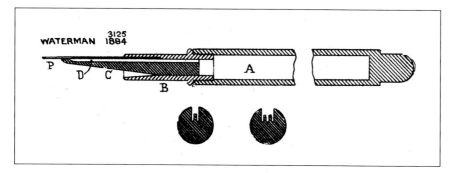

Waterman's first fountain pen: the two cross-sections through the ink feed show the capillaries for air and ink supply.

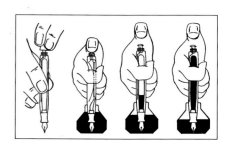

Parker's pressure filler and how it worked: Push the button, count to ten, let go--and the pen is filled.

Advertisement for Sheaffer's new Touch-Down fountain pen of 1949.

Eyedropper: The eyedropper filling system used the barrel to hold the ink. The earliest pens used this system. The section was simply unscrewed from the barrel and taken off. Then one eyedropped the ink into the barrel. This system originated in the nineteenth century. Almost all the older British and American firms started with it (Waterman, Parker, etc.).

Push Filler: This system is similar to the button filler, but the end cap cannot be unscrewed completely (Montblanc).

Vacumatic: Invented by Parker. Pens using this system could pull up 102% more ink than the customary systems of the time. Otherwise, this system was again similar to the button filler, but with a considerably greater ink capacity since the barrel was used to hold the ink.

Touch Down: The end of the barrel is unscrewed, and then pushed up and down to pull up the ink. Sheaffer used this system from the forties to the sixties.

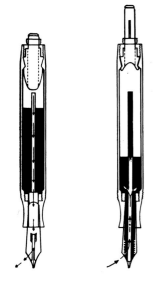

"Believe it or not"! Parker's Vacumatic filler could take up 102% more ink than pens with previous systems. Above, a cross-section of Parker's Vacumatic: When the button is pushed, a vacuum is created in the barrel, into which ink is pulled through a tube in the ink feed.

Leverless: This system was used by Swan in the thirties. As in the lever filler, there was a rubber bladder in the barrel, which was compressed by turning the end of the barrel and was emptied of or filled with ink. Unlike the lever filler, the leverless system did not use a lever.

History of the Montblanc Firm

In 1908, the "Simplo Filler Pen Company" was founded in Hamburg. The registration stated: "Manufactors of High Class Gold and Fountain Pens"; this name already included the firm's slogan that stressed quality. The partners were August Eberstein, Alfred Nehemias, Max Koch and Claus Johannes Voss. In 1909 Simplo's first fountain pens were put on the market. They were called "Rouge et Noir", and were safety pens in which the point was screwed out for use and then screwed back in when finished. At the same time eyedropper pens were also made. After unscrewing the section, the barrel was filled by means of an eyedropper.

"The flight over ideas...", Montblanc's well-styled advertisement for an elegant product.

No sooner was the firm founded than branches were opened in Paris, London and Barcelona. In 1909 the partner Max Koch left the firm; Christian Lausen entered the company in his place. In the same year, Alfred Nehemias died of a heart attack during a business conference in Paris. In 1910, Wilhelm Dziambor, who had already gained experience in the writing-goods industry, entered the firm in his place. In the same year, the first "Montblanc" fountain pens were made. The star symbol was registered as the firm's trade mark in 1913. In 1914 the firm was renamed "Simplo Füllfeder Gesellschaft". In 1919 Ernst Rösler entered the firm, and the first "Montblanc" specialty shop was opened by the Stöffhaas brothers. In 1921, Mr. Illgner, who had been the factory manager until then, left the company and founded his own "Astoria" firm, which was bought by Montblanc in 1932. In 1934 the firm was renamed again, and from then on it was called "Montblanc Simplo GmbH".

Lever fillers were also produced from 1921 to 1929. In 1924 the "Meisterstück" (Masterpiece) was put on the market, with a lifetime guarantee, in the same year as the compressor filler--a type of lever filler but with a barrel without a slit. But it was not a success on the German market and therefore is not noted in the list of the firm's products. In 1928 the first colored Masterpieces were produced.

In 1929, Montblanc put its first button fillers on the market, and in 1933 the Pix pressure pencil was introduced. Pencils had been tried as early as 1924, but they had not succeeded, on account of their complex mechanism.

In 1934 the first piston filler appeared--though Montblanc claims to have tested it as early as 1921. Now the Masterpiece series was made as piston fillers. In 1938 the rest of their pens were converted to piston fillers. In 1935, Claus Johannes Voss died, and K. Voss, Junior took his place in the business. Wilhelm Dziambor retired in 1936, and his son replaced him in the firm. In 1937 Ernst Rössler became a partner.

In 1947, Montblanc opened a factory in Denmark, where the button filler system was used for the most part. For that reason, there are many otherwise identical Montblanc models with different filling systems, depending on where they had been manufactured. Production in Denmark continued until 1957.

In 1952 the first ballpoint ink pens, the forerunners of the later roller-ball pens, were introduced.

In 1955, Montblanc put the winged point (as used in the 252, 254 and 256 models) on the market. The Masterpiece series, in practically the same form as used today, also sold with great success. There were four sizes: 142, 144, 146 and 149 (see page 11). In addition, they were produced in various colors, as well as with a rolled-gold cap (642 and 644), a silver-plated cap (also as 642 and 644), and fully gold filled and 14-karat gold form (both listed as 742 and 744). Today only three sizes are being made (142, 144 and 146). Along with the classic "Meisterstück", an additional Masterpiece series, comparable in design to the later "Classic Series" but fitted with a hidden 18-karat gold point, was introduced in 1959. This pen was numbered 12 and 14 (see page 16) depending on its size, and was also available with a gold filled cap (72 and 74), fully gold filled (82 and 84), and in 14-karat gold (92 and 94). To complete the range, matching pencils and ballpoint pens also could be bought.

In 1973 the "Noblesse" was introduced. This pen was an oddity in the firm's assortment, as it is made completely of metal.

In 1977, Dunhill acquired the majority of Montblanc shares. Dunhill took over the remaining shares of the old company in 1985, and in 1988 the firm's complete assortment was limited to the higher price range. School pens such as the Carrera series, and everyday pens such as the S-Line and Noblesse, were dropped and not replaced. Montblanc continued to produce chiefly the "Meisterstück" line, in sterling silver, gold filled and solid gold (Solitaire), and the Classic model. The new Noblesse series was introduced, but had little in common with the old line.

In 1991 the "Montblanc de la Culture" Foundation was established. In 1992, it offered a prize in the form of an 18-karat fountain pen. This prize is given once a year to artists who have achieved noteworthy success in the realms of art, music, theater or literature. The same type of pen that is given as a prize is offered in the trade by Montblanc, though not in gold, but rather in sterling silver or in vermeil, (gold plated sterling silver). On account of their sales success, these limited-issue fountain pens are accompanied by other limited series (see the chapter "Limited-Edition Fountain Pens") page 31.

The Montblanc Numbering System

Until 1929, the safety pens were numbered sequentially from 00 to 12, with this number indicating the pen's size. The following sizes were made: 00, 0, 1, 2, 3, 4, 5, 6, 7, 8, 10 and 12. The suffix k stood for the short and lg for the long version.

Until 1934, the safety fillers were numbered as follows: 12.5, 12.5k--15--17.5k and 19.75.

From 1932 to 1934, the low-priced 3rd Series was added, with a, b and c versions.

The Masterpieces were numbered 20, 25, 30, 35, 40 and 45 until 1934.

From 1935 to 1947, three-digit numbers were used.

The first digit meant:
1. Masterpiece
2. Second quality
3. Student pen
4. Stylograph

The second digit meant:
0. Safety filler
2. Button or push filler
3. Piston filler

The third digit meant:
2. Pen size

The following suffixes were used:
E. Rose pattern
G. Smooth
P. Pearl gray
PL. Silver gray/black
S. Guilloched

Thus, for example, the number 122PL indicates that the pen is a Masterpiece with push filling system, second size, with silver gray and black marbleized finish.

Since 1948, only piston and cartridge fillers have been produced in Germany. The three-digit numbering system still is used today, and has been extended by a fourth and a second sequence of digits:
1. Masterpiece
2. Second quality
3. School pen
6. Masterpiece with gold plated cap
7. Masterpiece in solid or 14-karat gold.

In the second numbering type, such as 12, the first number indicates the series (Masterpiece) and the second shows the pen size.

In most cases, the numbers appear on the filling mechanism, while in late models (since the fifties), one also finds the number on the cap band.

History of the Parker Firm

The former teacher and later company president George S. Parker in his office.

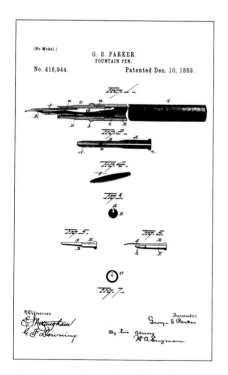

On December 10, 1889, George S. Parker received the patent for his first fountain pen.

The Parker Pen Company was founded in Janesville, Winsonsin in 1888 by a teacher named George S. Parker, who was dissatisfied with the quality of the fountain pens on the market at that time. Parker received his first patent on December 10, 1889. It applied to his new fountain pen and its ink feed. The most interesting Parker patent of those times is probably that of January 9, 1894. On that day, Parker registered his "Lucky Curve" ink feed for a patent. The special feature of this ink feed was that it curved under the section, so that the ink could flow back into the barrel. Thus a more even flow of ink was assured.

The first fountain pens were "systemless" in principle, meaning without their own filling system. When the section was withdrawn or unscrewed, the ink was put into the barrel by means of an eyedropper. In 1900 a variation of this type came on the market. Instead of removing the section for refilling, one simply withdrew the point along with the ink feed. These models are called "jointless". They were made in the most varied versions, for example, as the "Red Ripple", with the barrel ribbed in spiral form, or of aluminum with decorations, or in hexagonal form, or the pen was decorated with gold bands. Special models for doctors (with integrated thermometers) were also sold.

In 1916 both the "Button Filler" and the "Jack Knife" were introduced. The first "Duofold" fountain pens were placed on the market in 1921. These were still made of hard rubber and lacked cap bands. The first colors that were introduced were orange and black in the senior size. In the course of the following years, other colors and sizes were added. As of 1923, the Duofold pen also had cap bands. Parker offered a 25-year guarantee on these models.

In 1923 the "Vacumatic" was introduced. In comparison to the "Duofold", it could hold 102% more ink. With this series there first appeared the Parker arrow clip, which is still used today in slightly modified form. The arrow clip became an identifying mark of Parker pens. Usually the "Vacumatic" pens are found ringed in colors (gold, silver, red, green or blue); they could also be had in black or marbleized. The lifetime guarantee was also extended by Parker to the "Vacumatic".

In Britain and Canada, a variety of colorful fountain pens of the "Parkette", "Challenger", "Premiere", "Televisor" and other series appeared in the thirties and forties. Some of them are very hard to find today. The "Parkette" was Parker's only lever filler. It was made in both round and, as the "Parkette de Luxe", twelve-sided versions.

In 1941 the "51" came on the market. Its typical characteristic was the covered point--up to this time there had been, for the most part, only large free-standing points. Several firms followed this example and also put pens with covered points on the market in answer to the "51". The first "51" pens still used the Vacumatic filling system. In 1951 they were converted to the "Aeromatic" converter system.

In 1954, the first Parker ballpoint pen--the "Jotter"--went on sale. Unlike the present-day type, it had a rippled barrel, and the cap did not bear the arrow clip. The "61" fountain pen was also introduced in the fifties. Like the "51", it had a covered point, but in the section there also was a gold filled or silvered marker. The "61" was the first and only fountain pen to use the capillary filling system. On the ink feed there was a fixed cartridge which filled itself when it was held in the ink. This system did not work well, and therefore the Parker "61" remains the only pen with this filling system.

In 1966 the Model "65" appeared; it was filled with ink cartridges, and the point was again free-standing.

For the occasion of the moon landing in 1969, the "TI" was produced in 1970, but its production was so laborious and expensive that it was taken out of production in 1971. This series was made out of titanium. By adjusting a screw on the ink feed, one could modify the ink flow from light to heavy. Thus every user could always have the kind of writing he desired. This user-friendly characteristic too was found on only this one model.

The first Parker "75" came on the market in 1964. In 1966, Parker offered a special limited edition of this pen, for which a particular marketing idea had been developed. The special edition was made of the silver salvaged from the treasure fleet that had sunk in 1715. Only 4821 examples were produced, and this pen is appropriately expensive today.

On the other hand, the "75" series stayed in production for many years and was Parker's flagship model until the introduction of the "Premier" in 1985, but it remained in production, parallel to the "Duofold" series first issued in 1988, and was taken out of production only in 1994.

Italian Parker advertisements from various magazines.

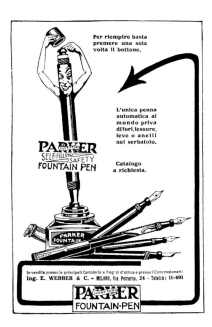

In 1978 Parker put the "180" on the market. Its special feature was the point that could be used from either side, allowing wide or narrow writing. This pen was available in extra fine-medium and fine-broad combinations. This series also went out of production later.

In 1992 the "Insignia" series appeared, but it consisted only of a ballpoint pen and a pencil.

In 1993, Parker set new accents in style and design with the "Sonnet", but this series was also reminiscent of the firm's long-gone models. With the "Sonnet", Parker is turning back to the legendary "51" model, which won the success in its day that the "Sonnet" has partially gained today and continues to strive for.

Parker's Advertisement for its "Duofold: fountain pen, with which the company gave a 25-year guarantee (see page 17).

History of the Pelikan Firm

What later became the "Pelikan" firm was founded in Hannover by Carl Hornemann (born 3/29/1811, died 12/13/1896). The firm came into being on April 28, 1838; this date is accepted today as the official beginning of the firm, since the firm's first printed price list appeared on that day. In addition to 76 water-color and oil paints, prepared oils and varnishes, it offered colored inks. For some years before that, Hornemann had been producing water-color pigments. On October 14, 1863, Günther Wagner, the man who gave the firm the name of Pelikan, became a partner. Soon he bought out the Hornemann family, buying the company in 1871.

The seventies brought "Pelikan" the financial upswing that other businesses also enjoyed after the victorious war with France. Wagner invested in machines and did a lot of advertising. In addition, he founded a second factory in Eger, which then still belonged to Austria. In the eighties, Fritz Beindorff came into the firm. At first he worked under Wagner's leadership; he even became Wagner's son-in-law; in 1894 he became a partner in the firm and as of January 1, 1895 he was the sole proprietor.

He founded twelve Pelikan branches in Eastern Europe and Latin America, and was part of the firm for almost sixty years. At the beginning of his career, he had 39 fellow workers; in 1888 (on Pelikan's fiftieth anniversary), there were already 62 employees. At the turn of the century in 1900, 236 employees held secure positions. In 1913 (the firm's 75th anniversary), there were 975 people working for Pelikan. In 1918, when World War I ended, there were 1110, while in 1928, at its 90th anniversary, the number of employees had grown to 2488. And in 1938, at the firm's hundredth anniversary, Pelikan had 3701 employees!

In 1863, when Günther Wagner joined the firm, the sale of ink already made up a great part of the firm's business. From then on, the sales catalog was divided into two parts, the first part including everything that painters, architects and engineers needed for drawing and students required for drawing lessons; the second part included the glues, stamp pads and all the other things used in the office. In 1897 the production of Pelikan inks began. Since 1900 Pelikan Oil, an adhesive that is still in production, has been made. In 1904 the first Pelikan typewriter ribbons were produced. Tinplate paint boxes were added in 1905, and the production of carbon paper was taken up in 1907. The firm has produced drawing pads since 1907. In 1929, one of Pelikan's most important dates (and surely for every Pelikan collector as well), writing instruments were also made for the first time. The first Pelikan fountain pen was the "100" model. It was made in black, black with a band set off in green, marbleized green (the entire pen), or, among others, marbleized in blue (see the large photo in the price guide). The somewhat striking versions are extremely hard to find today, since many

Generations of school children grew up with Pelikan ink. The firm's unmistakable label and the shape of the bottle, with the groove to hold the pen make it easily recognizable.

The birthplace of Pelikan.

of them were destroyed in the war. The versions with yellow or white gold coatings are extremely rare.

In 1932 Pelikan put the "Ibis" on the market. It usually turns up at sales today as a collector's item, in black, but there were also marble-ized versions. For export it was produced only in black, as the "Rappen". It was, of course, intended as a low-priced school pen, but to get a marbleized "Ibis" today, one has to pay many times what one would pay for a modern school pen.

In 1934 Pelikan produced the "Toledo", structurally identical to the "100" model but with 24-karat gold decoration on the barrel in the form of an artistically hand-decorated pelican. This pen is being made again today in two sizes, one in plain sterling silver, the other in gold plated sterling silver. In 1934 too, production of refillable pencils be-gan. The first model was black and marked "auch Pelikan". Later the same model, made to match the pens and with a green band, came on the market.

Pelikan introduced the "100N" in 1937. It differed from the previ-ous series in having a somewhat larger ink reservoir. In addition, the shape was changed somewhat. The piston was no longer rippled now, but smooth, with a conical end. This model was also available in every possible color variation; again, the simple black or black and green versions are found most often, as some colors were produced only for export.

In 1950 the legendary Pelikan "400" was produced; with the same model number and slightly changed shape, it is still available today. First available in seven versions, it is offered today in only two. But there also were expensive variants of it, namely the "500" model with gold filled piston and cap, or the completely gold filled "520".

In 1952 the Pelikan "140" was put on the market as the little brother to the "400". This series had equally conical pistons and cap ends. Just like its forerunner, it was available in many versions. The rarest colors are white and mother-of-pearl.

In 1955 the shape of the "400" was changed slightly, and it was called "400N" from then on. One year later, in 1956, it was changed a second time; the piston and cap end were now very pointed, and now it was called "400NN".

To match the pens, Pelikan built the appropriate pressure pencils. But there also were versions that could not be matched directly with a series of fountain pens, and remained individual items.

We might mention here the pencil with probably the most unusual mechanism that was ever built was the "Model 60". Instead of pushing the cap button or twisting the entire cap, it was bent! By bending the pencil, the lead supply was pushed outward. This pencil was available in green and in black. Since the pencil was very small, it could be filled only with 25 mm leads of 1.18 mm thickness. The normal lead length was 50 mm, sometimes only 35 mm. The standard lead thick-ness then was 1.18 mm; today, on the other hand, leads of 0.5 mm and 0.7 mm are chiefly required and produced.

Familienwappen Günther Wagner

The family coat of arms of Günther Wagner and the Pelikan emblem as it changed over the years.

The "Model 60" pencil was bent to push out the lead.

Parts of the Pelikan Pencil No. 50

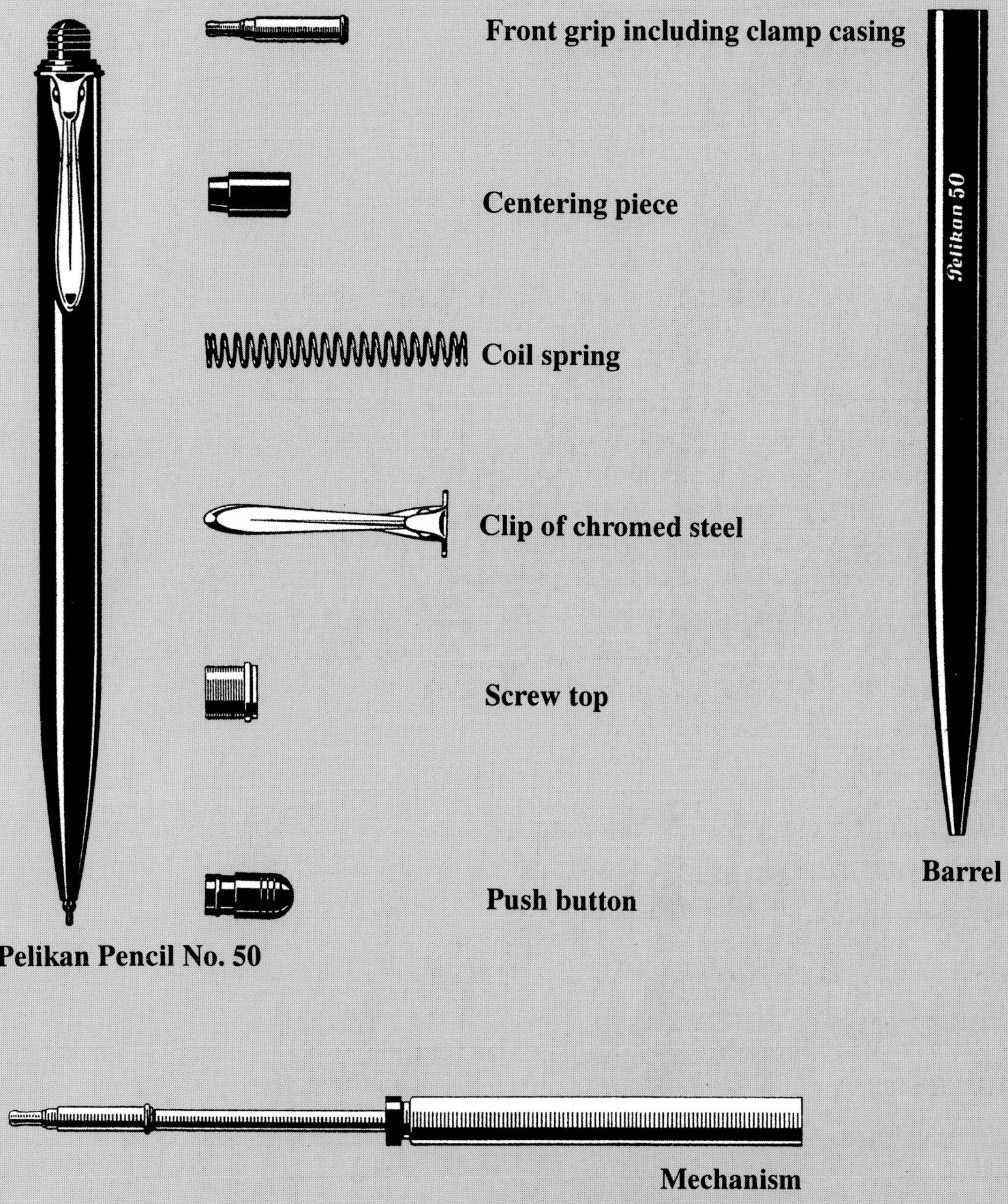

Front grip including clamp casing

Centering piece

Coil spring

Clip of chromed steel

Screw top

Push button

Pelikan Pencil No. 50

Barrel

Mechanism

In 1959 the "P1" was put on the market in eight different variations; this was a fountain pen that had a small, covered point. Until that time, all the points had been large and free-standing. The "P1" also was heavily advertised because of its flight safety and its elegant shape--it was slimmer than the other models.

The "Pelikano" school pen was introduced in 1960. Like the "P1", it had a covered point; at this time, other manufacturers also were selling fountain pens with covered points. The "Pelikano" was filled with a cartridge. To complete Pelikan's classic program, a whole series of pens appeared in the sixties, their designs reflecting the modern spirit of the times. Suddenly, stainless steel caps appeared on piston fillers, and the same models also appeared as cartridge fillers (Series 25). The clip, until then unmistakable in the shape of a pelikan's bill, was changed to a non-identifiable Pelikan clip (Series P30/M30 and P20/M20), with "M" indicating a piston mechanism and "P" standing for the cartridge filler.

Today a "P1" in good condition is hard to find, as it did not sell well, being more expensive than the classic "400". The "Green Stripes" were classic then, as they are now.

The modern "25" and "30" are not very interesting to collectors.

This love for nostalgic writing instruments was surely the reason why Pelikan included in their program, or as special issues, the "400" (14-karat gold point) as the Model "600" with an 18-karat gold or platinum-plated point, plus a decorative ring on the piston as well as on the cap, even issuing them in a masculine format as the "800" model. Recently the firm has also issued limited editions, such as the "Blue Ocean", selling only 5000 of them worldwide, and in 1992, the "800" in transparent green (3500 sold, though not in Germany). In September 1994 the "Hunting" appeared, a "Toledo" in green with a silver band on which a stag can be seen. The whole edition consisted of 3000 pieces, of which 600 have been reserved for Germany. The price was 1900 marks. The transparent ball-point pen to match the "800" was also issued in America. 700 were made.

W.A. Sheaffer

Crest™ Collection

Sheaffer Headquarters, Fort Madison, Iowa

History of the Sheaffer Firm

Walter A. Sheaffer was born in Bloomfield, Iowa on July 27, 1867. He had already had numerous jobs before he could become his father's partner in the family's jewelry business. There, and later in his own jewelry business, he was able to develop his ability as a sales strategist further and further. When he decided in 1912 to take up the challenge of turning from a retailer into a fountain-pen manufacturer, he was already 45 years old.

The founder, president and manager W. A. Sheaffer had a thorough knowledge of the marketing and sales of high-priced merchandise. In fact, he possessed an infectious enthusiasm for deliberately selling nothing but high-quality products. This enthusiasm was spread to his employees and made sure that the newly-founded firm would attain success against the strong competition on the market.

The story began as follows: On an autumn evening in 1907, W. A. Sheaffer read an advertisement in a daily newspaper for a "Conklin" fountain pen, which was filled with ink by means of a half-moon-shaped ring on the side of the barrel by pressing on a rubber reservoir. Many fountain pens at this time were sold as "eye-droppers" or were filled with ink by pressing with a coin through a slit in the barrel. W. A. Sheaffer's idea was that there must be a system that worked without disturbance and without the laborious mechanism of the "coin-filler". A few days later he had found the solution. He dispensed with the eye-dropper by inserting an air-removing rubber sack in the barrel of the pen. He eliminated the unattractive crescent that sat on the pen like a hump, and inserted a lever in the coin slit, so as to draw ink into the rubber sac by pressing on it. The lever was designed so that it fit smoothly into the flat slit in the pen, and thus the first practical lever filler was invented.

Sheaffer registered his first patent in 1908, and this patent was to change America's writing habits! As a cautious merchant, and despite all his enthusiasm, he took his time about series production and the actual step into the market. Only in 1913 was the Sheaffer Pen Company founded in Iowa. W. A. Sheaffer remained the firm's president for twenty-five years, but even after his retirement he remained active in the firm's activities until his death in 1946.

In 1938, his 41-year-old son Craig R. Sheaffer successfully took his place as the new president of the firm. This new, strong and innovative leadership heightened the firm's success. Since the first hand-made fountain pen, produced in his father's workroom at the onetime jewelry store, Craig had been familiar with the fountain-pen business. Only in 1953 did Craig Sheaffer leave the business for one year, upon being named Secretary of Commerce in the cabinet of the newly-elected President Eisenhower. But in 1954 he returned to the family business, where he remained the head of the firm until his death on July 9, 1961.

In 1914, the first Sheaffer advertisement was published in the Saturday Evening Post. In his very first year in business, Sheaffer already gained 3% of the writing-equipment market and could already achieve sales of over $100,000, the profit representing 50% of the original investment. In 1914 the firm moved into a former creamery building in Fort Madison, the building standing on Front Street, opposite the Mississippi River. Later the building was used for research and developmental purposes; today it serves as a storehouse.

In 1918 the first Sheaffer pencil, the Sharp Point, was produced.

In 1920 the first fountain pen with a lifetime guarantee appeared on the market. The pens sold for prices beginning at $8.75, this being three times the price of the competing products. For that price, the purchaser received a lifetime guarantee for the pen--which was unparalleled at that time.

In 1924 the white dot was introduced as a trade mark. It is now used as the symbol of the lifetime guarantee. In 1925, Sheaffer had increased its share of the market to 25%. One of the most outstanding innovations made by the firm in the twenties was the development of pens made of plastic, bringing the hard-rubber era to an end. The plastic material could be colored better and made possible pens in a wide variety of colors.

In 1929, the "Balance" series was introduced, a line of models with a conical shape to the barrel and cap ends.

In 1930, the pen-and-pencil combination came onto the market, a writing device that combined fountain pen and pencil in one object.

In 1942, Sheaffer introduced the "Triumph" series, which is still made today in a slightly changed form.

The firm's first ball-point pen was produced and marketed in 1946. It shows a further development by Sheaffer, namely the clip mechanism that is still in use today. The point was pushed in and out by pressure on the clip. The "Touchdown" fountain pen is likewise a development of the forties.

In November 1951, the fifty millionth Sheaffer fountain pen came on the market! In 1952 the "Snorkel" was introduced; here the point no longer came into contact with the ink. In 1959, the "PFM" (Pen for Men) appeared, this being a series for the gentleman, with the same filling mechanism.

The firm's first cartridge filler appeared in 1961, and in 1963--for its fiftieth anniversary--there was a cartridge filler with a "lifetime" guarantee.

In 1966, the converter was offered as an alternative to the cartridge.

In 1976, the "Targa" series came onto the market.

In 1979, Sheaffer conquered the French market. Sheaffer writing instruments are now sold all over the world (in more than 150 countries). To support its worldwide sales, branches have been opened in Belgium, Holland, Germany, Italy, Hong Kong, Malaysia, Japan and Singapore.

In 1980, Sheaffer reintroduced the "Nostalgia", a classic pen from the twenties.

In 1985, the "Connaisseur" was introduced and remained for seven years the firm's flagship along with the "Nostalgia", being replaced only in 1992 when the "Crest" came on the market.

History of the Waterman Firm

The year was 1884. Lewis Edson Waterman applied for a patent for his first workable fountain pen. It was called "Ideal" and was "pre-destined to satisfy the customer, or the sales price will be refunded!" (Waterman's sales slogan in 1885)

The Waterman firm was founded by Lewis Edson Waterman in 1883. L. E. Waterman was actually an insurance agent. But how does an insurance agent happen to found his own fountain-pen factory? This story goes as follows: One day, when Waterman was about to have a large contract signed, he gave a pen that had been usable until then to his client to sign the contract. When the client put the pen to the paper, a big pool of ink poured onto the paper. Before Waterman could prepare a new contract, his client signed a contract with another agency. Waterman decided to produce fountain pens himself--pens that would not leak. The result was the "Ideal" pen. It was then made only in black. Waterman himself sold all 72 of his fountain pens in 1883! In the following year, on February 12, 1884, he patented the capillary system in the ink feed, which he had invented. This ink-filling system was remarkably simple. The point was unscrewed and ink was poured into the barrel. The feed provided a smooth, even flow of ink. In 1894 Waterman personally sold 500 fountain pens, each with a five-year guarantee. Thanks to their good quality, five-year guarantee and re-

Advertisements ranging from Art Nouveau to Art-Deco were often created very deliberately in the style of Japanese woodcuts.

peated advertising in the journal "The Review of Reviews", he had already increased his turnover tenfold by 1887, and because of the quickly growing business, Waterman no longer visited all his customers himself. The business expanded. In 1888, the firm of

L. E. Waterman & Co. was founded in New York at 155 Broadway. In 1890, the firm's first writing set was introduced. In 1898, Waterman expanded his range to include five more fountain pens, now offering a variety of models. In 1899, Waterman celebrated a world "premiere": a 14-karat gold pen with a very broad point went into production.

In 1900, the firm's agent, William I. Ferris, invented a machine that made the production of fountain pens quicker and easier. Later Ferris was responsible for the construction of new factories in New Jersey and Seymor, Connecticut. With successful sales in Canada, a factory also was built in Montreal. A company journal, the "Pen-Prophet", was published. It was intended for stores selling pens and provided them with information about writing instruments, new products, promotional activity and much more.

Lewis Edson Waterman died in 1901 at the age of 64, and his nephew Frank D. Waterman took over the leadership of the firm. At this point, 350,000 writing instruments had already been produced, and the first exports to Europe were made. Since 1896, pens with gold and silver decorations were produced.

In 1907, Waterman introduced the "Safety" fountain pen to the market. The point was extended for writing and screwed back inward afterward. Because of a solidly closing cap, the pen was leakproof. In 1907, a lot of advertising was undertaken; ads appeared in about 200 different papers and magazines in the months of November and December alone. On December 2, 1907, the firm's advertisements reached 1000 different cities! At this time, the Waterman assortment included about a hundred different fountain pens.

Waterman put its first lever filler on the market in 1915. On the side of the barrel was a lever that had to be pushed upward when one wanted to fill the pen. The point was held in the ink bottle. Under the lever was a rubber ink sac. When the lever was raised, a panel pressed on the sac and suction was created. This process was repeated three or four times and the sac was filled.

All the Waterman writing instruments had a logical numbering system. For example, the number "42" meant that the pen was a safety type. The first number indicated the ink-filling system, and the second showed the size of the point.

Since 1914, the Frenchman Jules Fagard possessed the sales rights for Waterman fountain pens in Europe. They were now sold all over the world. In 1926, Fagard founded the firm of "Jif Waterman" and produced writing instruments himself.

"Red Ripple" fountain pens were introduced in 1923. Being of different sizes and versions, they were made of hard rubber and had an interesting pattern.

In 1927, an employee of the Jif Waterman firm, M. Perraud, invented the ink cartridge. In 1935, Jif Waterman obtained the worldwide patent and built an ink factory in a suburb of Paris.

The "Patrician", probably the most interesting writing instrument of that era, appeared on the market in 1929. It was available in five colors and two sizes (for men, and for ladies as the "Lady Patrician"). In 1992 the men's version of the "Patrician" was issued anew in three colors.

In 1939, Waterman put its "100-year-pen" on the market. The firm gave a hundred-year guarantee on the unbreakable cap and barrel! The point was also marked with "Hundred Year" lettering.

Just one year later, in 1940, the first fountain pens made of steel were produced. In that year Madame Fagard took over the leadership of the firm when her husband died.

The first four-color ball-point pen, the "Pantabille", appeared in 1947.

In 1953, a chief stylist of the General Motors firm designed the "CF" pen. "CF" stands for Cartridge Filling. The pen's shape was innovative for the fifties, for other firms were still putting pens with small covered points on the market, and this was the absolute opposite. The point of the "CF" was not covered and reached high up to the container, similar to the present-day "Edson".

In 1954, production of writing instruments by Waterman USA came to an end. Jif Waterman obtained the rights and continues to produce in France. For the collector, the American-made Watermans are more interesting.

In 1963, the "Maxima" ball-point pen was introduced.

In 1965, the firm's leadership changed again, after the death of Mme. Fargard. Her daughter, E. Le Foyer, took on the management.

In 1967, a new factory was built in St. Herblain; production continues here to this day.

In 1969, the daughter of E. Le Foyer, Francine Gomez, took over as director of the company.

In 1975, after various sales of marketing rights had taken place, Waterman had a turnover of 94 million francs, 26 million of which came from the exporting of writing instruments.

In 1982, all Waterman writing instruments took on the same appearance. The double clip was introduced.

In 1983, the "Man 100" was introduced for the hundredth anniversary of the firm's founding.

In 1992, the "Edson" was introduced in France. Since 1993 it has also been available in Germany. It is marked by a new point shape and technical as well as optical features that have been used for the first time in this fountain pen as well as the firm's ball-point pens.

In 1993, Waterman was taken over by the Gillette group.

In 1994, Waterman moved its company headquarters to Baden-Baden. Since then, its logistics have been combined with those of Parker.

The Waterman Numbering System

As of 1898, Waterman gave its fountain pens a unified numbering system, by which one could tell definitely what kind of filling system the pen had, whether it was made of gold or gold filled, etc. For the collector who can decode this system, it also makes it possible to determine whether the pen is in original condition or has been modified after being made. The numbering system consists usually of four digits, which can also have one or more letters added. This system was used with minor revisions until the end of the thirties.

The number in the thousands position means:
0 = Pen is gold filled
1 = Pen has a slim 14-karat gold cap band
2 = Pen has two 14-karat gold bands, one at the upper end of the   cap, the other at the end of the barrel.

The number in the hundreds position means:
2 = Pen has a silver covered barrel
3 = Pen has a gold filled covered barrel
4 = Pen has a silver cap and barrel
5 = Pen has a gold filled cap and barrel
6 = Pen has a mother-of-pearl barrel (after 1917, the "6" meant   that the pen had two gold bands on the barrel)
7 = Pen has a 14-karat gold band on the barrel
8 = Pen has a 14-karat gold band on the cap
9 = Pen has a 14-karat gold band on the upper end of the cap

The number in the tens position means:
0 = straight cap
1 = Conically tapering cap
2 = Pointed cap
3 = Pen in vest-pocket format (used only until 1908)
4 = Pen for desk set (after 1917, 7 = safety pen)
5 = Lever filler
6 = Lever filler with push cap
7 = Eyedropper pen with screw cap
8 = Pump filler (mechanism similar to piston filler)

The number in the final position shows the point size. The following point sizes have existed: 2, 3, 4, 5, 6, 7, 8, 10.

Additional indications:

1/2 = Pen is thinner

X = Larger barrel than usual for this point size

V = Pen is shorter

SF = Self filler (lever filler)

S = Safety filler

P = Pump filler

POC = Pocket format

PSF = Self filler, pocket format

VP = Vest pocket format

For example, if one has a Waterman fountain pen with the number

4 5 2 1/2

one can identify this pen precisely as follows:

-- the thousands place is empty

--4 = Pen has silver cap and barrel

--5 = Lever filler

--2 = Point size

--1/2 Pen is thinner than the usual size

This is very important information for the collector. If some feature of the pen does not correspond to this information, then one can assume that the pen is no longer in original condition!

As of 1928, Waterman fountain pens were also made to which this numbering system did not correspond.

There was a special feature of the Waterman number 7 model. The pen was equipped with a color code that was reflected in color at the upper end of the cap. The color indicated the width of the nib.

Pink = Flexible fine point, also for shorthand

Purplish-red = Stiff fine point

Brown = Fine point, non-scratching

Red = Standard point, medium width

Green = Stiff medium point

Yellow = Round point, also for lefthanders

Blue = Short, easily tilted pen

Limited Edition Pens

Montblanc

In recent years, more and more fountain pens have been marketed in limited editions. The leader in this area is the firm of Montblanc, which in conjunction with the awarding of the annual cultural prize "Montblanc de la Culture" awards a special fountain pen to three people once a year and also issues the awarded model in series. In 1992 the first of the limited editions, the "Lorenzo di Medici", was introduced with a worldwide production of 4810 pieces and a price of 2500 marks. The reason for it to be so named was the 500th anniversary of the death of the famous member of the Medici family. In Germany, 522 of these pens were sold.

Ernset Hemingway, above, and Agatha Christie were among those who gave their names to Montblanc limited editions.

In the same year, the "Hemingway" appeared, a "Masterpiece" in black and orange, blending old styling elements with new and named after the author Ernest Hemingway. Thirty thousand of these pens were produced, of which 1800 pieces were intended for the German market. The fountain pen cost 950 marks, and with a little luck, one can still find it in the shops today. It was accompanied by a pencil (480 marks).

In 1993, the "Octavian" was chosen to sell at a special price. Again, the complete issue numbered 4810 pieces and the price was 2500 marks. Of these, 509 pieces were sold in Germany. This model was named in honor of the Roman emperor Octavian. The pen is decorated with a spiderweb of 925 silver.

Another limited edition, with a price of below 1000 marks apiece, was offered to the collector in 1993. The pen was named "Agatha Christie" in honor of the great mystery writer who had achieved world-wide renown through her works. The pen is a "Masterpiece" in black, with a sterling silver snake clip in which two genuine rubies represent the eyes. The number of these pens made added up to 30,000, the individual price was 985 marks. There was also a matching ballpoint pen (25,000 made) and a pencil (7000). Two thousand of the fountain pens were sold in Germany, 1600 of the ballpoint pen, and 700 of the sets-- ballpoint pen and pencil--were reserved for the German market. The pencil was available only in the set, which cost 495 marks. As a special treat, this series was also available with gold clips, at a price of 1350 marks. The total number made was 4810, of which 435 of the pens were reserved for Germany.

The "Imperial Dragon" was developed especially for the Asian market. Unlike the "Christie", it had, instead of the snake clip, a clip in the form of a dragon. In the standard version, with dragon clip of sterling silver, it had a production run of 5000 fountain pens, 3500 ballpoint pens and 1500 pencils. There were also 888 pens made with 18-karat gold dragon clips. All of these were sent to Asia. Forty-eight of them came back to Germany in 1994 and were divided among four specialty shops. The German price was 2500 marks, oriented to the Asian sales price.

The next limited-edition fountain pen made by Montblanc appeared in 1994; it was the "Louis XIV", named after the Sun King. Eighteen-karat gold versions of this pen were given to the three 1994 prizewinners. The model available in the trade sells for 2700 marks and is made of 925 silver with 23.5-karat gold plating. The pen is decorated with a flower pattern intended to remind one of the flowery decor of the festival halls in the palace of Versailles. By August 1, 1994, 456 of them had been sold in Germany.

In the autumn of 1994, the next limited "Masterpiece" was introduced. This time it was named after Oscar Wilde. The eccentricity of his life style is reflected in this fountain pen, which is very unlike the usual designs. The pen has a green-white-black marbleized pattern; 15,000 fountain pens, 8000 ballpoint pens and 5000 sets were made.

Pelikan

Pelikan also issues limited editions of fountain pens. The first of them, the "Blue Ocean", appeared in December 1993. It is physically identical to the regular 800 series except for being transparent blue. The complete edition numbered 5000 fountain pens and 1000 sets, the latter consisting of fountain pen and ball-point pen. Of these, 1000 pens and 300 sets were reserved for the German market. The same model had appeared in transparent green in America some two years earlier; this issue numbered 3500 pens which sold for $450. The price of the "Blue Ocean" in Germany was 780 marks for the fountain pen and 1100 marks for the set.

In September 1994 the "Hunting" appeared, a fountain pen in 800 series format, based on the "Toledo" but made in green with a silver ring on which a classic hunting motif--a bellowing stag--is shown. The edition was limited to 3000 pieces worldwide, of which only 650 were reserved for Germany, where they sold for 1900 marks.

Parker

Parker issued its first limited-edition fountain pen as early as 1966. This was the "75 Treasure Pen", made from silver salvaged from the treasure fleet that sank in 1715. Kip Wagner, an antique dealer, salvaged this silver treasure over a period of more than ten years and then sold a portion of the silver coins to Parker, who used the silver to produce the fountain pens. The pen bears the name "Treasure Pen". 4821 were produced.

Around 1971, another fountain pen of the 75 type was introduced as a limited edition; this was the "Queen Elizabeth", of which 5000 were made of brass.

The next limited-edition fountain pen came on the market in 1976. It was made of pewter, and its special feature was the piece of wood worked into the top of the cap, a relic of Independence Hall in Philadelphia. The issue numbered 10,000 pieces.

The "Wood Pen" Series of fountain pens was produced in and for Germany in 1982. In all, only 2000 pieces were produced out of eight different kinds of wood.

Duofold fountain pens with sterling silver decorations are produced in America. One of them is the "Spiderweb", a fountain pen covered with a spiderweb pattern. These, though, are not official productions by Parker, but are produced and distributed in other ways.

In the sixties, as it did in the thirties, Parker distributed the "Holy Water Sprinkler", a fountain pen that is not officially limited, but it may be presumed that only a small number of these pens were produced.

Waterman

Waterman has also issued writing instruments in limited editions. In 1989, a fountain pen and ballpoint pen appeared, based on the "Man 100" series but, unlike the normal issues, was made with a small plaque on the clip. The series was occasioned by the 200th anniversary celebration of the French Revolution. The cap inscription read: "Bicentenaire de la Revolution Française". The clip plaque shows three birds and the years 1789-1989. This series was produced only in 1989. The number of pens made is not known, but it could scarcely have been more than ten thousand.

Fisher

Fisher, the firm with the first pen in space, issued a titanium-alloy version of the "Space Pen" in the summer of 1994. The occasion was the 25th anniversary of man landing on the moon. Accordingly, the ballpoint pen was equipped with a small plaque. The issue was limited to 20,000 pieces, each accompanied by a separate certificate. The ballpoint pen itself was not numbered, and the sales price was thus only 49 marks.

Most limited-edition writing instruments are numbered, often with the total issue also stated. But there are also writing instruments that are numbered but not limited. More and more often, the manufacturers are also numbering their upper-level standard issues. This is supposed to express exclusivity and give the customer the impression that their pen is unique. And so it is, at least to the extent that there is only one pen with that particular number! In addition, it can always be determined where the pens were shipped and sold.

Personal Tips for Collectors

By which criteria does one best build up his collection? At this point it is appropriate to start with a few basic ideas in mind (see "Aspects of Collecting"). If one wants to collect from a historical perspective, then the gathering of various writing utensils itself will do, but if one wants to assemble a valuable collection, involving an investment, that is no longer possible in the usual manner. Let it be said here that a mixture of all those possibilities can be achieved through sensible and well-planned collecting.

Since the collecting of writing instruments has become very popular only recently, one can still start with some material that has been tucked away and not yet offered to the public--items that are still sleeping in various drawers and just waiting to fall into the loving hands of a collector. Thus the first collecting place of every collector must be the immediate family. Another rewarding source can be a small advertisement in regional weekly papers or antique journals. My advice: Do both! Alternatives that remain for the advanced collector are auctions. At auctions there is often the disadvantage of being bound to buy large lots although one may be interested in only one pen. In addition, long-range bidding does not let you check the condition, and getting one's money back often proves to be difficult. Christie's and Bonham's auction houses in London are sources of valuable writing instruments.

As sources for the collector, we must also mention antique shows and flea markets. One seldom finds high-quality writing instruments there, but rather a quantity of writing instruments. Every collector can find something to meet his individual needs.

After you have gathered a number of specimens together, you probably face the problem of repairing and polishing. You can easily carry out the second item yourself. Silver or plastic polish works. Using it, you can bring almost any material to a high polish. Polishing machines are optimal, but they are not cheap. Surely everyone ought to know a friendly shoemaker who might let you use his machine.

The repairing of writing instruments, insofar as one values a functioning fountain pen, is usually the most difficult thing. Often one needs replacement parts, which are only available by "cannibalizing" a similar pen. Before making a purchase, you should consider well whether the pen is worth the cost of repairing it, for an original point from the thirties, for example, can be more expensive than the whole pen. In general, you should clean every pen and rid it of any traces of ink. Tap water is suitable for this job. If you have filled a fountain pen and not used it for a long time, wash it out with clear water. Black ink in particular likes to clot after a certain time, and then cleaning it is all the harder.

Storage: For a small number, it is handy to keep them in their own boxes, when available. But with about twenty or more pens, this can result in chaos.

As an alternative, I recommend grooved boards, which can probably be purchased in small writing-goods shops for a few dollars if they are no longer needed. For the advanced collector, or for anyone who goes to collectors' meets, there are boxes that can be bought which, according to their size, can hold more than forty pens. For storage at home, one should keep the value of the collection in mind and protect it accordingly. The customary insurance on household goods can be extended to include collections; their insurance value can be upgraded by a certain percentage. With a collection worth more than 30% of the insured value of the household goods, one ought to buy a safe.

I wish you a great deal of happiness in collecting!

Regina Martini
Birkerfeld 16
51429 Bergisch-Gladbach
Germany

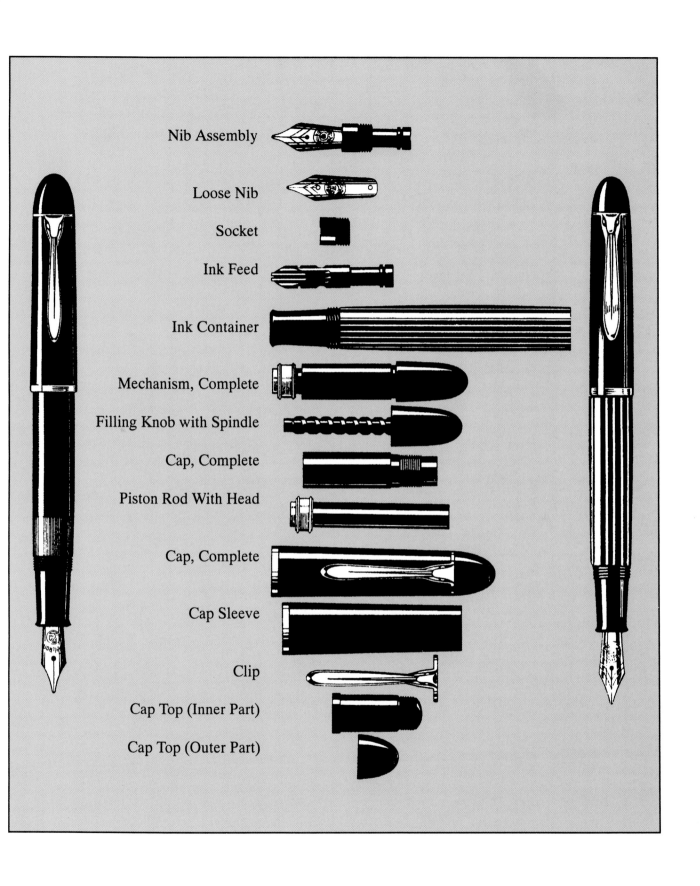

Nib Assembly

Loose Nib

Socket

Ink Feed

Ink Container

Mechanism, Complete

Filling Knob with Spindle

Cap, Complete

Piston Rod With Head

Cap, Complete

Cap Sleeve

Clip

Cap Top (Inner Part)

Cap Top (Outer Part)

KAISERLICHES PATENTAMT.

PATENTSCHRIFT

— № 268152

KLASSE 70b. GRUPPE 4/30

AUSGEGEBEN DEN 8. DEZEMBER 1913.

HEIDELBERGER FEDERHALTER-FABRIK KOCH, WEBER & CO. IN HEIDELBERG.

Füllfederhalter mit vor- und zurückschiebbarem Schreibfederträger.

Patentiert im Deutschen Reiche vom 21. Dezember 1912 ab.

Die bekannten Füllfederhalter mit vor- und zurückschiebbarem Schreibfederträger, bei denen das Verschieben des Schreibfederträgers und Tintenleiters durch eine mit einem Schrauben-
5 gang versehene Hülse erfolgt und seine Geradführung durch eine Nut in dem Tintenbehälter oder durch eine oder mehrere schraubengangförmige Nuten im Tintenbehälter geschieht, haben den Nachteil, daß ein Vor-
10 wärtsschieben des Tintenleiters so weit erfolgen kann, daß eine Schädigung des Halters oder Leiters hervorgebracht wird. Dieser Übelstand soll nach der Erfindung ohne Verwendung von Brems- oder Reibungsgesperren
15 vermieden werden, deren Wirkung bekanntlich von Federn oder Pressungen abhängig ist. Nach der Erfindung mündet die der Führung des Stiftes dienende gerade oder schraubengangförmige Nut in eine Ringnut, in welche
20 der Stift am Ende seiner zulässigen Bahn, d. h. sobald der Abschlußkegel die Schließlage eingenommen hat, eintritt. Es wird daher der Kegel in der Schließstellung gehalten. Eine weitere Drehung des Tinten-
25 leiters oder des mit ihm verbundenen Drehknopfes hat dabei keinerlei Einfluß auf den Vorwärtsgang des Tintenleiters.

Auf der Zeichnung zeigen:
Fig. 1 einen Längsschnitt durch den neuen
30 Füllfederhalter, der Tintenleiter ist in der zurückgezogenen Stellung gezeichnet,

Fig. 2 einen gleichen Schnitt, der Tintenleiter befindet sich hier in vorgeschobener Stellung, und
Fig. 3 einen Längsschnitt durch einen Füll- 35 federhalter in anderer Ausführungsform.

Die bekannte Führungsnut i läuft in eine im Zylinder herumlaufende Nut k aus (Fig. 1 und 2). Diese Führungsnut i verhindert die Drehung des Stiftes c und somit des Tinten- 40 leiters b, so daß bei der Drehung der Hülse f lediglich eine Längsbewegung des Tintenleiters eintritt. Unmittelbar nachdem der Tintenleiter gegen den vorderen Anschlag m trifft, tritt der Stift c in die Ringnut k ein, so daß 45 ein Überdrehen vollständig ausgeschlossen ist, denn beim Weiterdrehen der Hülse f wird sich der Stift c lediglich in dieser Ringnut k herumdrehen, ohne daß ein weiteres Vorwärtsbewegen des Tintenleiters eintreten kann. 50

Das Zurückziehen des Tintenleiters erfolgt in bekannter Weise durch Rückwärtsdrehen der Hülse f, wobei der Stift c aus der Ringnut k wieder in die Längsnut i übergeht, sobald der Stift c die Stelle erreicht, an der 55 die Nut i in die Nut k übergeht. Dieser Übergang kann in beliebiger Weise, beispielsweise durch besondere Gestaltung der Ringnut oder durch federnde Ausbildung der betreffenden Teile erzwungen werden. 60

Bei der in Fig. 3 dargestellten Ausführungsform wird das Vor- und Rückwärtsbewegen

durch zwei im äußeren Mantel a angebrachte schraubengangförmige Nuten e' bewirkt, welche nach oben in eine Ringnut k' enden. Der Tintenleiter b besitzt hier zwei Stifte c', welche
5 sich in geradlinigen Schlitzen der Hülse f' führen. Diese Schlitze entsprechen dem Schlitz i in der ersten Ausführungsform und sind auf der Zeichnung in Fig. 3 nicht sichtbar. Die Wirkungsweise dieses Halters entspricht genau
10 dem nach Fig. 1 und 2, da nur eine Umkehrung des Schraubenganges e und der Geradführung i mit Bezug auf die Hülse f und den äußeren Mantel a vorgenommen worden ist.

Statt der in den beiden gezeichneten Aus-
15 führungsformen beschriebenen Ringnut k, k' könnte man auch den Schraubengang e in Fig. 1 an der Stelle aufhören lassen, in welcher der Tintenleiter an den Anschlag m

stößt, so daß der Stift c in dieser Lage durch den zylindrischen Teil der Nut e oder das 20 Ende der Hülse f geführt würde.

PATENT-ANSPRUCH:

Füllfederhalter mit vor- und zurück- 25 schiebbarem Schreibfederträger, bei dem das Verschieben des Schreibfederträgers und Tintenleiters durch eine mit einem Schraubengang versehene Hülse erfolgt und seine Geradführung durch eine Nut in dem Tin- 30 tenbehälter geschieht oder durch eine oder mehrere schraubengangförmige Nuten im Tintenbehälter, dadurch gekennzeichnet, daß die zur Führung des Stiftes (c) dienende gerade oder schraubengangförmige Nut $(i$ 35 bzw. $e')$ in eine Ringnut $(k$ bzw. $k')$ mündet.

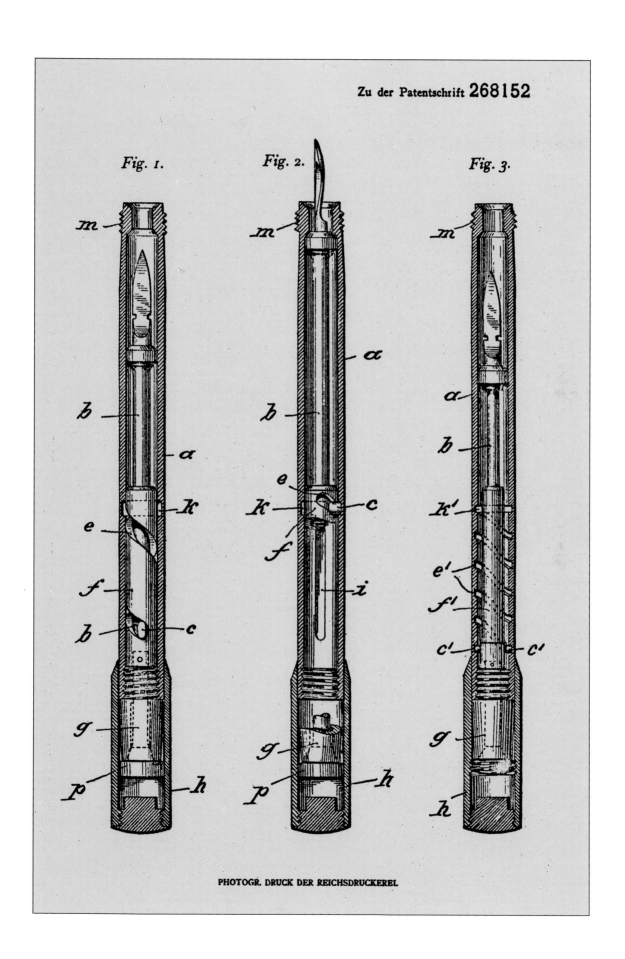

Fig. 1.   Fig. 2.   Fig. 3.

PHOTOGR. DRUCK DER REICHSDRUCKEREL

Catalog Section

The frequently used abbreviations

Abbreviation	Meaning	Further Details
9K	9-karat = 375 gold	Customary in Britain
14K	14-karat = 585 gold	Customary in Germany & the United States
15K	15-karat = 625 gold	Customary in Britain
18K	18-karat = 750 gold	Customary in Italy & France
Duo	Duofold	Parker
FT	Flat Top	Sheaffer & Parker
LP	Retail price as of 8/95	
MB	Montblanc	
No.	Number	
Vacum.	Vacumatic	Parker

Note: When an illustration shows several pens, they are described in order from left to right or from top to bottom.

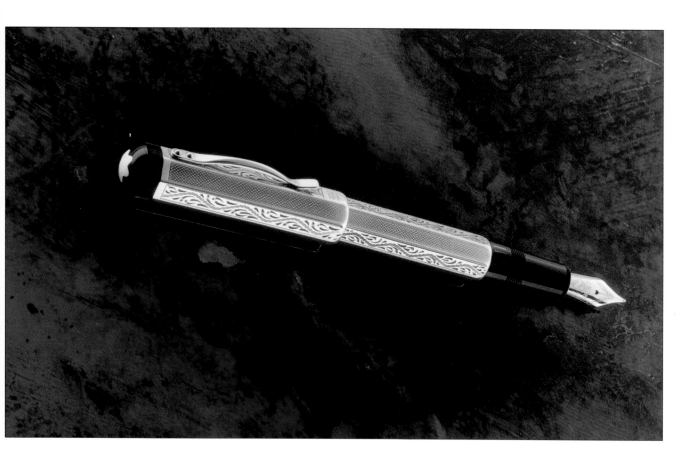

Limited Editions
Montblanc

Lorenzo de Medici 1992 $3500-4000
Sterling Silver

Hemingway fountain pen 1992   LP $600-700
orange/black
Hemingway ballpoint pen 1992   LP $300-400
orange/black (not shown)

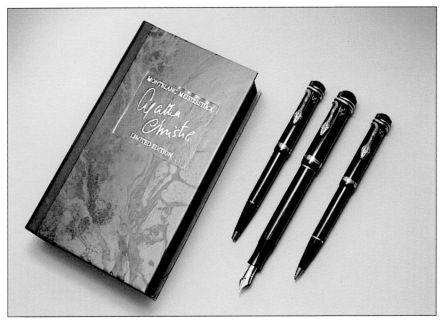

Agatha Christie fountain pen 1993 LP $500-600
Sterling silver snake clip
Agatha Christie ballpoint pen 1993 LP $300-350
Sterling silver snake clip
Agatha Christie pencil   LP $200-300
1993, Sterling silver snake clip
Agatha Christie fountain pen 1993 $600-700
Gold snake clip (not shown)

Octavian 1993 $2200-3000
Sterling silver

Imperial Dragon fountain pen $3500-4500
1993, 18-karat gold clip
Imperial Dragon fountain pen $1800-2100
1993, silver clip (not shown)
Imperial Dragon ballpoint pen 1993 $700-800
Silver clip (not shown)
Imperial Dragon pencil $600-650
1993, silver clip (not shown)

Louis XIV 1994 $2000-2500
Gold plated silver

Oscar Wilde fountain pen 1994   LP $500-700
green/white/black marbled
Oscar Wilde ballpoint pen 1994   LP $250-350
green/white/black marbled

Limited Editions Pelikan

800 fountain pen ca. 1991 $500-600
transparent green
800 ballpoint pen 1994 $150-200
transparent green (not shown)
Blue Ocean fountain pen 1993 $500-600
transparent blue
Blue Ocean ballpoint pen 1993 $200-250
transparent blue
Hunting fountain pen 1994 $1000-1300
green/silver band

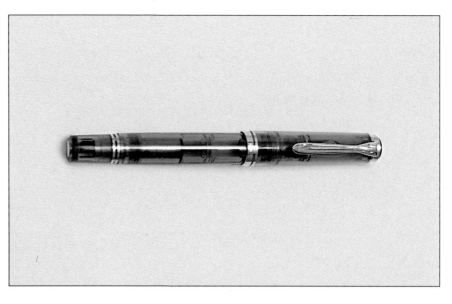

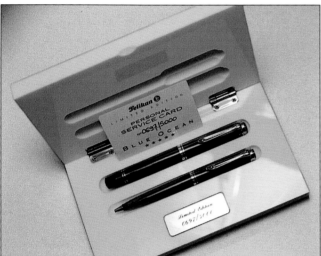

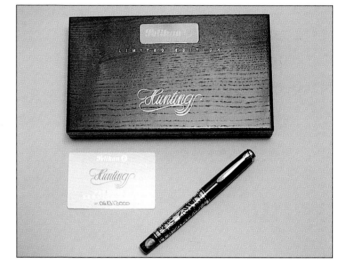

Limited Edition Fisher

Fisher Space pen 1994
titanium alloy $30-45

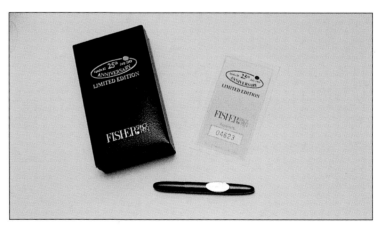

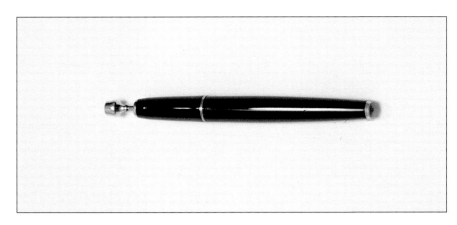

Holy Water Sprinkler $300-350
ca. 1965, sprinkles holy water

75 Treasure Pen 1966 $900-1100
Sterling silver

75 Pewter 1976 $450-600

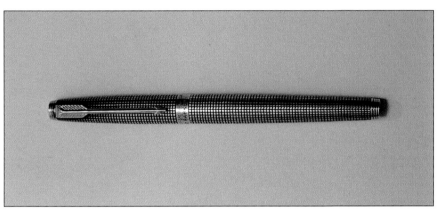

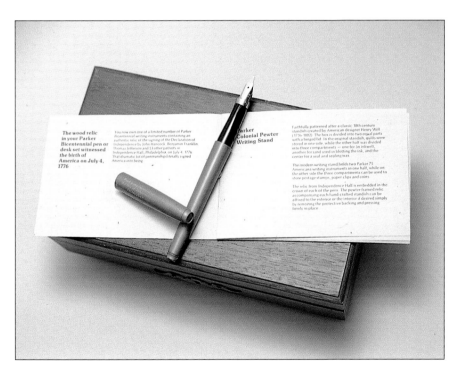

Wood Pen Bruyère 1982	$300-500
Wood from North Africa	
Wood Pen Pockholz 1982	$300-500
Wood from Jamaica	
Wood Pen Partridge 1982	$300-500
Wood from Central America	
Wood Pen Peru Palisander	$300-500
1982, wood from Peru	
Wood Pen Königsholz	$300-500
1982, wood from Brazil	
Wood Pen Grenadill 1982	$300-500
Wood from Tanzania	
Wood Pen Cocobolo 1982	$300-500
Wood from Nicaragua	
Wood Pen Cocus 1982	$350-600

Wood from the Dominican Republic

The wood from the Dominican Republic was prohibited from being exported soon thereafter. For that reason, considerably fewer of this Wood Pen were produced.

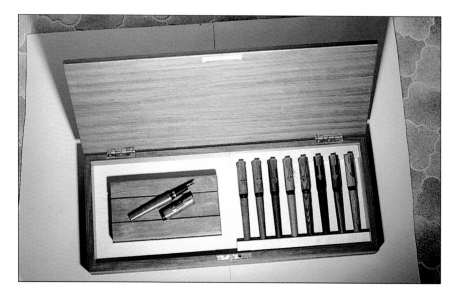

Limited Editions Parker, Waterman

Parker Spiderweb 1992	$1775
Silver, spiderweb pattern	
Parker Butterfly and Flowers	$1775
1994, silver with flowers	
Parker Art Moderne 1994	$1775
Silver, Art Deco	
Parker Windows 1994	$1775
Silver, Gothic windows	
Parker Hand Engraved	$1775

1994, silver, floral decor (not shown)
1000 of the Spiderweb and 500 of each of the others were made. All the pens were private productions making use of the Duofold.
All versions also exist in 14-karat gold; 100 of each were issued. Collectors' price $3550 apiece.

Waterman Man 100 fountain pen	$285
1989, black (not shown)	
Waterman Man 100 ballpoint pen	$145
1989, black	

Burnham

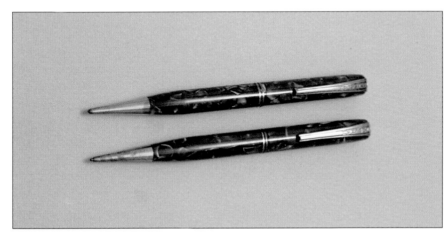

The Burnham ca. 1935	$100-120
Red Ripple	
Pencil ca. 1950	$16-20
blue/gold marbled	
Pencil ca. 1950	$16-20
green marbled	
Pencil ca. 1950	$16-20
red marbled (not shown)	
Pencil ca. 1950	$16-20
gray marbled (not shown)	
Pencil ca. 1950	$16-20
black (not shown)	
No. 44 ca. 1950	$16-20
black	
No. 44 ca. 1950	$20-30
red/gray marbled	
No. 44 ca. 1950	$20-30
green marbled (not shown)	
No. 44 ca. 1950	$20-30
blue marbled (not shown)	
No. 48 ca. 1950	$30-40
green marbled	
No. 48 ca. 1950	$30-40
green marbled	
No. 48 ca. 1950	$30-40
red marbled (not shown)	
No. 49 ca. 1950	$16-20
gray	
No. 49 ca. 1950	$20-30
blue marbled	
No. 50 ca. 1950	$30-40
black	
No. 56 ca. 1950	$16-20
black	
No. 65 ca. 1950	$30-40
black	

Conway Stewart (1905-1975)

No. 36 ca. 1950 red striped	$35-50
No. 36 ca. 1950 green striped	$30-35
No. 36 ca. 1950 black (not shown)	$30-35
No. 58 ca. 1950 blue marbled	$75-85
No. 58 ca. 1950 green (candy stripe)	$75-85
No. 58 ca. 1950 gray (candy stripe) (not shown)	$75-85
No. 58 ca. 1950 gold/brown marbled (not shown)	$35-45
No. 58 ca. 1950, black	$35-45
No. 388 ca. 1950 blue marbled	$35-45
No. 388 ca. 1950 brown marbled	$34-45
No. 388 ca. 1950 green marbled	$35-45
No. 388 ca. 1950 red marbled	$30-35
No. 388 ca. 1950 black	$30-35

No. 85 L ca. 1950 red marbled	$60-8
No. 85 L ca. 1950 green marbled (not shown)	$60-8
No. 85 L ca. 1950 blue/gold	$80-1
No. 85 L ca. 1950 blue (herringbone)	$90-1
No. 85 L ca. 1950 green (herringbone) (not shown)	$90-1
No. 85 L ca. 1950 black	$35-5
No. 84 ca. 1950 red marbled	$65-7
No. 84 ca. 1950 blue marbled	$65-7
No. 84 ca. 1950 green marbled (not shown)	$65-75
No. 84 ca. 1950 green/blue marbled (not shown)	$65-75
No. 84 ca. 1950 green/gold marbled	$80-9(
No. 84 ca. 1950 blue/gold marbled	$80-9(
No. 84 ca. 1950 black	$35-50
No. 27 ca. 1950 blue marbled	$90-10
No. 27 ca. 1950 green marbled (not shown)	$90-10
No. 27 ca. 1950 black	$50-60

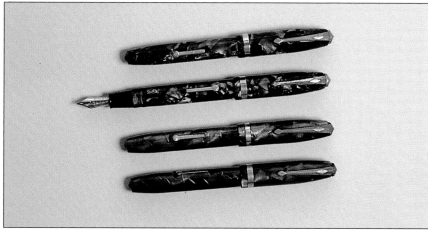

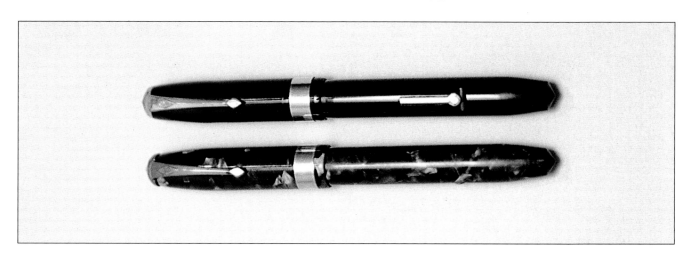

No. 15 ca. 1950	$35-40
blue marbled	
No. 15 ca. 1950	$35-40
green marbled	
No. 15 ca. 1950	$35-40
red marbled	
No. 15 ca. 1950	$20-25
black (not shown)	
No. 75 ca. 1950	$70-80
blue marbled	
No. 475 ca. 1950	$90-100
blue marbled	
No. 73 ca. 1950	$90-100
blue marbled	
No. 759 ca. 1950	$90-100
blue	
No. 286 ca. 1950	$40-55
green marbled	
No. 286 ca. 1950	$40-55
blue marbled	
No. 286 ca. 1950	$40-55
gold marbled	
No. 286 ca. 1950	$20-25
black	

No. 330 ca. 1935	$40-50
Scribe in black	
No. 356 ca. 1935	$35-40
International, black	
No. 200 ca. 1935	$50-60
black	
No. 28 ca. 1950	$60-70
brown (tiger-eye)	
No. 28 ca. 1950	$60-70
(candy stripe)	
No. 466 ca. 1950	$50-60
red marbled	
No. 60 Executive ca. 1950	$80-100
red marbled	
No. 67 ca. 1960	$15-20
red/stainless steel	
No. 104 ca. 1960	$15-20
red	

Dinkie 550 ca. 1950	$30-40
blue marbled	
Dinkie 550 ca. 1950	$30-40
green marbled	
Dinkie 550 ca. 1950	$30-40
red marbled	
Dinkie 550 ca. 1950	$30-40
blue/brown marbled (not shown)	
Dinkie 540 ca. 1950	$30-40
blue/gold marbled	

Nippy ca. 1940	$18
green marbled	
Nippy ca. 1940	$18
blue marbled	
Nippy ca. 1940	$18
red marbled (not shown)	
Nippy ca. 1940	$10
black (not shown)	
Duro Point No. 2 ca. 1940	$30
light green marbled	
Nippy No. 3 ca. 1950	$18
red marbled	
Nippy No. 3 ca. 1950	$18
blue marbled (not shown)	
Nippy No. 3 ca. 1950	$18
green marbled (not shown)	
Nippy No. 3 ca. 1950	$10
black (not shown)	
No. 25 ca. 1950	$18
red marbled	
No. 25 ca. 1950	$18
blue marbled	
No. 25 ca. 1950	$18
green marbled (not shown)	
No. 25 ca. 1950	$10
black (not shown)	

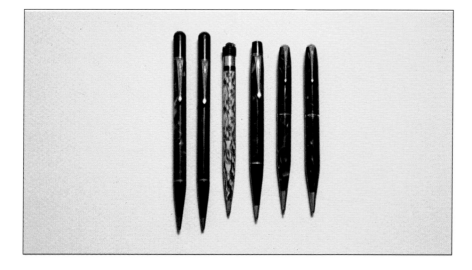

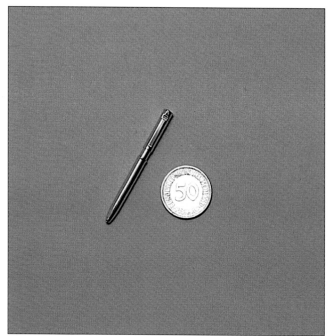

Diplomat
(1922 to date)

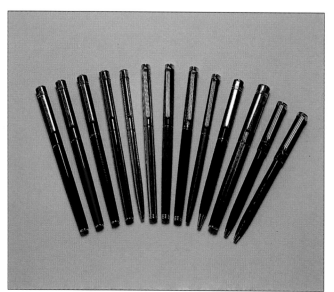

Diplomat ballpoint ca. 1950, black	$5
Diplomat ballpoint ca. 1960, black/gold filled cap	$5
Diplomat ballpoint ca. 1960, brown/gold filled cap	$5
Diplomat pen ca. 1960, black/aluminum cap	$5
Diplomat 76 ballpoint ca. 1960, red striped	$8
Diplomat 22 pen ca. 1960, red striped	$22

In 1981 Diplomat was taken over by the firm of Imco J. Michaelis. The complete line of products was changed.

Attaché pencil gold filled 1992	LP $35

Smallest mechanical pencil in the world.

Attaché pen Stratos 1990, blue glazed	LP $55
Attaché pen Sierra 1992, rose-red painted	LP $55
Attaché pen Midnight 1989, black guilloche	LP $60
Attaché pen Gun Metall 1989, charcoal gray	LP $55
Attaché ballpoint Chrom ca. 1988, chromed	LP $48
Epoque pen Chrom ca. 1988, chromed	LP $68
Epoque pen Ind. Summer 1992	LP $95
orange marbled	
Epoque pen Gun Metall ca. 1989, charcoal gray	LP $82
Epoque ballpoint Titan ca. 1989, titanium-enriched	LP $125
Lord ballpoint Marmor blau 1992, blue marbled	LP $60
Lord pen Gun Metall ca. 1989, charcoal gray	LP $82
Embassy ballpoint 1993, black painted	LP $42
Embassy ballpoint 1993, green marbled	LP $56

Esterbrook
(1933-1971)

Relief No. 1 ca. 1935	$40-50
black	
Esterbrook 1938	$25-30
mother-of-pearl red	
Esterbrook 1938	$20-30
black	
Esterbrook ca. 1960	$20-30
red	
Esterbrook ca. 1960	$20-30
black	

Classic Marmor ballpoint	LP $75
1992, green marbled	
Classic Tabac FH	LP $110
ca. 1989, brown marbled	
Classic Marmor ballpoint	LP $75
ca. 1990, blue marbled	

Esterbrook 1950 gray	$10-20	**Esterbrook** 1950 blue speckled	$20-30	**Esterbrook** 1950 mother-of-pearl gray	$25-35
Esterbrook 1950 green	$10-20	**Esterbrook** 1950 black	$15-20	**Esterbrook** 1950 black	$20-30
Esterbrook 1950 mother-of-pearl blue	$20-30	**Esterbrook** 1950 mother-of-pearl green	$25-35	Esterbrook produced this series in five sizes.	

Fend

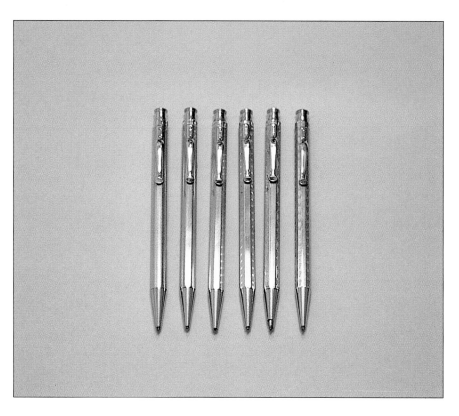

Normix pencil ca. 1950	$42
round, waved guilloche	
Normix pencil ca. 1950	$42
octagonal, waved guilloche	
Normix pencil ca. 1950	$42
stripes and waves	
Normix pencil ca. 1950	$55
stripes with N pattern	
Normix pencil ca. 1950	$55
Waves with art deco	
Normix pencil ca. 1950	$55
Stripes and angled waves	
All pencils are gold filled.	
Normix pencil ca. 1950	$22
900 silver	
Normix pencil ca. 1950	$15
silver-plated	
Truxa ballpoint ca. 1960	$15
silver-plated without clip	
Normix pencil ca. 1950	$30
900 silver	
Truxa ballpoint ca. 1960	$30
900 silver	
Truxa ballpoint ca. 1960	$22
silver-plated	
Normix pencil ca. 1950	$30
900 silver	

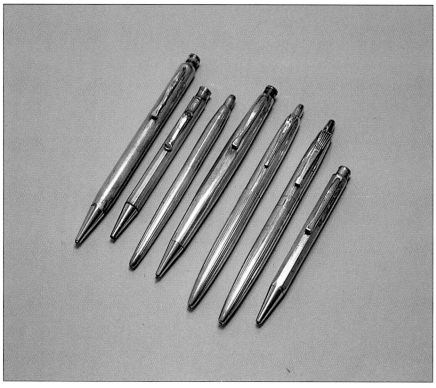

Opposite page, upper right:	
4-Color Truxa ca. 1950	$15
silver-plated	
4-Color Truxa ca. 1950	$22
rolled gold	
6-Color Norma ca. 1950	$30
silver-plated alpaca	
2-Color Super Norma	$30
ca. 1960, 900 silver	
4-Color Super Norma	$15
ca. 1960, silver-plated	
4-Color Fend ca. 1970	$8
chrome-plated	
6-Color Truxa ca. 1970	$22
chrome-plated	

Fend produced a great variety of multicolor pens, ballpoint pens and pencils with various patterns, but they all have similar values.

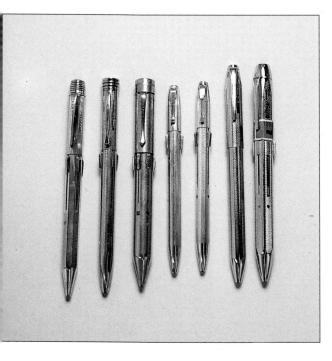

Geha
(1918-1991)

(Taken over by Pelikan in 1991)

Geha transparent ca. 1955	$70
demonstrator	
80 ca. 1955, black	$42
Regent 710 transparent	$90
ca. 1955, demonstrator	
Geha pen ca. 1955	$22
black	
Geha Schulfüller ca. 1955	$15
black	
Geha pen ca. 1955	$15
black	
60 pen ca. 1955	$35
black	
60 pen ca. 1955	$70
green stripes	
05 ballpoint ca. 1955, red	$15
05 ballpoint ca. 1955	$8
black (not shown)	
03 G pen ca. 1960	$8
aluminum/green	
Geha pen ca. 1965	$15
black	
Geha ballpoint ca. 1965	$8
black	
eans pen ca. 1983	$5
school pen, blue/black	

Kaweco
(1885-1970)

Kaweco No. 0310 pencil	$70
ca. 1920, Red Ripple	
Omega pen ca. 1910	$145
silver with enamel	
Kaweco No. 603 pen 1914	$110
black, safety pen	
Kaweco Spezial 68 pencil	$22
ca. 1925, black	

Omega was the best alternative to the Kaweco writing instruments. There were also silver-mounted Kawecos.

Kaweco Transparent	$70
ca. 1950, red marbled	
Kaweco Transparent	$70
ca. 1950, green marbled	
Kaweco Transparent	$70
ca. 1950, blue marbled	
Kaweco Transparent	$70
ca. 1950, gray marbled	
Kaweco Transparent	$70
ca. 1950, gold marbled (not shown)	
Kaweco 117 ca. 1960	$70
black/green lines	

Kaweco Sport 11 pen 1938	$35
black, smooth	
Kaweco Sport 12 pen 1955	$35
black, smooth	
Kaweco 18 pencil 1955	$18
black, smooth	
Kaweco ballpoint 1955	$18
black, smooth (not shown)	
Kaweco Sport pen 1955	$55
black, V guilloche	
Kaweco pencil 1955	$22
black, V guilloche (not shown)	

Kaweco Elite 183 a 1938 $35
black
Kaweco Elite 187 a 1938 $55
black
Kaweco Elite 190 a 1938 $70
black
Kaweco Kadett 45 a ca. 1945 $22
black
Kaweco Kadett 475 N $22
ca. 1950, black
Kaweco Colleg 55 a ca. 1950 $30
black
Kaweco Dia 802 1938 $70
green marbled
Kaweco Dia 802 1938 $70
red marbled (not shown)
Kaweco Dia 802 1938 $70
blue marbled (not shown)

Kaweco Dia 787 1938 $35
black
Kaweco Dia 85 a 1938 $35
black
Kaweco Dia 802 N ca. 1950 $35
black
Kaweco Dia 802 G ca. 1950 $55
red
Kaweco Dia 803 ca. 1950 $35
black
Kaweco Dia 805 G ca. 1950 $42
black

Kaweco 602 ballpoint 1965 $10
gray
Kaweco 607 ballpoint 1965 $8
black
V14 S pen 1965 $15
black/stainless steel

Lamy/Artus
(1930 to date)

Artus Ballit 42e 1961, black	$22
Artus Ballit 42 e 1961, wine-red (not shown)	$30
Artus Ballit 42 e 1961, blue-green (not snown)	$30
Lamy 99 1962, black	$22
Lamy 99 1962, red (not shown)	$30
Lamy 99 1962, blue (not shown)	$30
Artus Rekord 45 ca. 1963, black	$15
Lamy 27 n 1952, black/stainless steel	$8
Lamy 27 n 1952, blue/stainless steel	$8
Lamy 27 n 1952, red/stainless steel (not shown)	$8
Lamy 27 1952, demonstration model	$70
Lamy 27m 1952, black/gold filled	$30
Lamy 27n 1952, blue/gold filled (not shown)	$42
Lamy 27n 1952, red/gold filled	$30
Lamy 27 (30n) 1962, black, gold filled clip	$18

Kaweco pen 1970, turquoise marbled	$22
Kaweco ballpoint 1970, turquoise marbled	$8

Ratio 47 p 1962 $8
black/stainless steel

Ratio 47 p 1962 $8
blue/stainless steel (not shown)

Ratio 47 p 1962 $8
red/stainless steel

Ratio 46 1961 $10
turquoise

Ratio 46 1961 $10
black

Ratio 46 1961 $10
red (not shown)

Ratio 46 p 1961 $8
turquoise (not shown)

Ratio 46 p 1961 $8
black (not shown)

Ratio 46 p 1961 $8
red (not shown)

Ratio 49 f ca. 1960 $10
black

81 1973 $22
black/stainless steel

25 p 1969 $8
stainless steel/black

25 p 1969 $8
stainless steel/pink (not shown)

25 p 1969 $8
stainless steel/ochre

66 p 1971 $70
demonstration model

68 1971 $8
dark blue

68 1971 $8
black (not shown)

68 1971 $8
green (not shown)

26 1972 $10
stainless steel

86 1974 $15
black

Numerous models were available as both piston
and cartridge fillers. The letter "p" identifies
cartridge fillers.

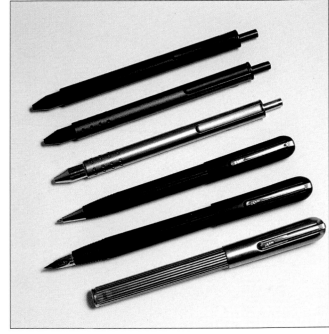

2000 (01) pen 1966, black	LP $110
Safari ballpoint 1981, green	$8
Safari ballpoint 1981, orange	$8
Safari ballpoint 1983, yellow	LP $12
Lamy Safari transparent ca. 1983, demonstrator	$35
Lamy CP 1 3-Color ballpoint 1979	LP $46
stainless steel, lined	
Lamy Unic ballpoint 1987, titanium alloy	LP $70
Lamy Twin Pen 1988, titanium alloy	LP $82
Lamy Sprit 1994, stainless steel	LP $27
Swift roller 1990, black	LP $35
Swift roller 1993, dark gray	LP $37
Swift roller 1990, titanium	LP $40
Persona ballpoint 1992, black	LP $138
Persona pen 1992, black	LP $230
Persona ballpoint 1992, titanium (not shown)	LP $210
Persona pen 1992, titanium	LP $300

Montblanc
(1908 to date)

1 Safety Pen 1924, octagonal, black		$200-225
154 Safety Pen ca. 1930, black		$150-175
302 Safety Pen 1935, black		$120-140
2 Safety Pen 1920, black		$150-175

Safety pens were made in point sizes from 00 to 12. Safety pens were also made in colors and with gold and silver plating.

Safety Pen, Stöffhaas, ca. 1925, black $110-125

Stöffhaas was the first Montblanc specialty shop that sold only products made by Montblanc.

Astoria ca. 1925, 18-karat gold filled $500-575

Astoria was founded in 1921 by the then Montblanc works manager and was bought out by Montblanc in 1932.

Montblanc

Masterpiece 20 1935, red	$225-250
Masterpiece 25 1935, red	$275-325
Masterpiece 30 1935, red	$350-400
Masterpiece 20 1935 black (not shown)	$175-200
Masterpiece 25 1935 black (not shown)	$200-225
Masterpiece 30 1935 black (not shown)	$250-275
Masterpiece 40 1935 black (not shown)	$400-450

1 pencil ca. 1925 black	$55
2 pencil ca. 1925 black	$55
5 pencil ca. 1940 black	$35
Kalender pencil ca. 1950 black	$35
Excelsior 924 ca. 1930 black	$35

Stöffhaas 230 ca. 1930 black	$35
MB 221 ca. 1930 black	$35
MB 320 ca. 1930 black	$35
MB 322 ca. 1930 black	$55
MB 324 ca. 1930 black	$70

Excelsior was a Montblanc subsidiary brand (founded 1913).

Models for the German market were also made in blue-gold, blue, green and maroon. Higher values apply to these models.
The German pens were marked with the name "Meisterstück", the Danish with "Masterpiece". The German pens were made up to size 45 between 1930 and 1931.

Meisterstück L 25 1931 $325-400
black and pearl
Meisterstück L 30 1931 $400-450
black and pearl
Meisterstück L 35 1931 $450-500
black and pearl (not shown)
The cap is usually in the same pattern as the barrel.
Also available in marbled green, marbled blue-gold and black.

No. 2 1935 $125-140
red (not shown)
No. 4 1935 $150-175
red
No. 6 1935 $175-225
red (not shown)
These models were produced in Denmark.

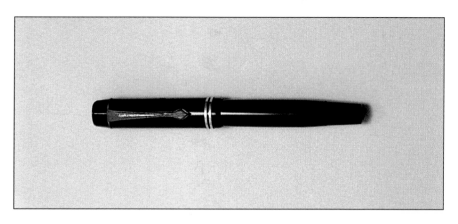

234 1/2 1936 $50-75
black

Stylo 432 1937 $70-80
black

Meisterstück K 132 1938 $150-175
black
72G Pix pencil 1938 $30-40
black
Meisterstück 132 1938 $150-175
black (not shown)
Meisterstück 134 1937 $175-200
black (not shown)
Meisterstück 136 1937 $225-250
black (not shown)
Meisterstück 139 1939 $400-450
black (not shown)
Meisterstück 138 1939 $300-325
black (not shown)
Meisterstück 136 ca. 1947 $325-400
black

The Meisterstück pens were also available as
122, 124, etc. (1935-1938); these were press
fillers, while those listed above were piston
fillers.

2 K ca. 1940, black	$22
2 ca. 1925, black/red	$35
0 1935, black	$22
2 Pix 1935, black	$22

No. 32 also exists in other color combinations, matching the ink color.

72 Pix ca. 1945, black	$35
4 ca. 1945, black	$35
92 Pix 1950, black	$22
73 Pix 1956, black	$35

02 1950, red	$135-150
04 1950, red	$150-175
06 1950, red (not shown)	$175-200
02 1950, black	$50-75
04 1950, black (not shown)	$75-100
06 1950, black	$100-125

212 1950, red		$75-110
214 1950, red (not shown)		$100-140
216 1950, red (not shown)		$150-200
25 pencil 1950, red		$35-45
212 1950, black (not shown)		$50-75
214 1950, black (not shown)		$75-100
216 1950, black		$100-125
17 ca. 1945, red		$40-55
33 ca. 1945, red		$40-55
33 ca. 1945, red		$40-55
72/2 Pix ca. 1935, red		$65-85
40 1/2 ca. 1945, red		$40-55
242 1947, black		$100-135
244 1947, black		$135-160
246 1947, black		$160-185
242 1947, red (not shown)		$95-120
244 1947, red (not shown)		$100-140
246 1947, red		$150-200
46 pencil 1947, red		$50-70
244 1947, green marbled		$350-400
246 1947, green marbled		$450-500

These models are Danish press fillers; they were also made in marbled green.

242 1950 $110-150
black, piston (not shown)
244 1950 $125-175
black, piston
246 1950 $175-200
black, piston (not shown)

Meisterstück 142 1948 $135-150
black
Meisterstück 144 1948 $150-175
black
Meisterstück 146 1948 $175-200
black
Meisterstück 149 1952 $225-275
black (not shown)
Meisterstück 144 1958 $200-225
black, transitional model
Meisterstück 142 1955 $385-425
green striped
Meisterstück 144 1955 $400-450
green striped
Meisterstück 146 1955 $450-550
green striped (not shown)
172 pencil 1955 $110-125
green striped

There was also a black and white striped series.
Price increase by size: $70.

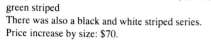

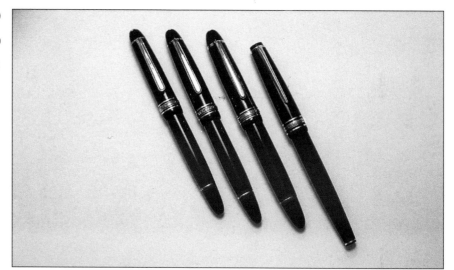

Meisterstück 642 1952	$200-250
green marbled/gold filled cap	
Meisterstück 642 1952	$185-225
green marbled/Silvexa cap	
Meisterstück 642 1952, black/gold filled cap	$185-225
515 ballpoint 1952, black/gold filled cap	$90-100
Meisterstück 644 1952	$250-300
green marbled/gold filled cap (not shown)	
Meisterstück 644 1952	$200-250
green marbled/Silvexa cap (not shown)	
Meisterstück 644 1952	$200-250
black/gold filled cap (not shown)	
Meisterstück 742 1952, gold filled (not shown)	$350-450
Meisterstück 744 1952, gold filled (not shown)	$400-500

742 and 744 also were available, with the same numbers,
in 14-karat gold.

252 1956, black	$55-75
252 1956, green	$90-110
252 1956, red	$90-110
254 1956, black	$70-80
254 1956, green (not shown)	$110-130
254 1956, red (not shown)	$110-130
256 1956, black	$145-175
256 1956, green (not shown)	$175-225
256 1956, red (not shown)	$175-225
276 Pix pencil 1956, black (not shown)	$35-45
276 Pix pencil 1956, green	$55-65
276 Pix pencil 1956, red (not shown)	$55-65
215 ballpoint 1956, black	$35-45
215 ballpoint 1956, green (not shown)	$55-65
215 ballpoint 1956, red (not shown)	$55-65
3-42 G 1958, black	$55-65
344 1958, black	$70-85
346 1958, black (not shown)	$110-125
376 Pix pencil 1958, black (not shown)	$22-30
342 1958, green	$70-80
344 1958, green (not shown)	$110-125
376 Pix pencil 1958, green	$55-75
342 1958, red (not shown)	$70-80
344 1958, red (not shown)	$110-125
376 Pix pencil 1958, red	$55-75

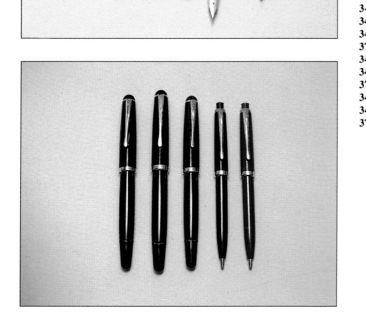

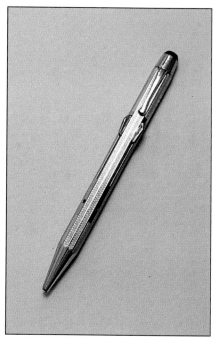

4-Color ballpoint ca. 1960	$35-40	**Montblanc** ca. 1965
chrome-plated		matte black

4-Color ballpoint ca. 1960 $35-40
chrome-plated

Meisterstück 12 1959 $55-65
black
Meisterstück 12 1959 $90-110
green (not shown)
Meisterstück 12 1959 $90-110
gray
Meisterstück 14 1959 $70-90
black
Meisterstück 72 1959 $110-125
black/gold filled cap
Meisterstück 74 1959 $145-175
black/gold filled cap (not shown)
Meisterstück 82 1959 $160-190
gold filled (not shown)
16 pencil 1959 $22-30
black
121 pen ca. 1960 $42-50
black
181 ballpoint ca. 1960 $22-30
black

Montblanc ca. 1965 $30-35
matte black
250 pencil ca. 1965 $8-10
matte black
Montblanc 220 ca. 1965 $35-45
matte black
Montblanc 126 ca. 1965 $55-65
black/925 cap

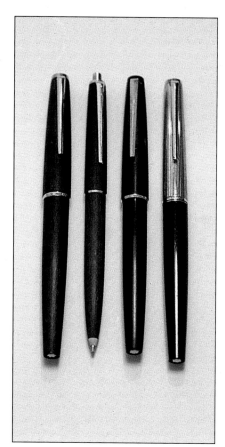

22 1959	$30-40	**221** 1959	$55-65
black		green	
22 1959	$42-50	**38 ballpoint** 1959	$15-20
red		black	
22 1959	$42-50	**251 pencil** 1959	$18-25
green (not shown)		black	
24 1959	$35-45	**28 ballpoint** 1959	$25-35
black		green	
31 1959	$22-30	**25 pencil** 1959	$25-35
black		red	
32 1959	$30-40		
black			
32 1959	$55-65		
red			
32 1959	$55-65		
green			
32 S 1959	$55-65		
black/silvexa cap			
34 1959	$35-45		
black			
221 1959	$35-45		
black (not shown)			

Monte Rosa 042 1958, black	$22-30
Monte Rosa 042 1958, lilac blue	$42-50
Monte Rosa 042 1958, green	$42-50
Monte Rosa ca. 1962, black/angled	$35-45
Junior 622 ca. 1965, black/stainless steel	$15-20
No. 49 S ballpoint ca. 1965, black/stainless steel	$8-12
Carrera pen ca. 1975, yellow/black	$35-40
Carrera pencil ca. 1975, yellow/black	$20-30
Carrera pen ca. 1975, black/stainless steel	$8-12
Carrera ballpoint ca. 1975, black/stainless steel	$5-8
Turbo ca. 1975, stainless steel	$8-12

All these writing instruments were low-priced student models.
The Monte Rosa was also available with gold or steel nibs.

Classic 1968, black, steel point	$22
Classic 1968, red, steel point (not shown)	$25
Classic black, gold point	$30
Classic 1968, red, gold point (not shown)	$32
Classic 1992, black (not shown)	LP $100
Classic 1992, red	LP $100
Noblesse 1973, sliver-plated	$22
Noblesse 1973, stainless steel, gold clip	$22
Noblesse 1968, titanium alloy	$50
Noblesse 1968, gold-plated	$55
Meisterstück 144 1985, black	LP $100
Meisterstück 144 1985, red (not shown)	LP $150
Meisterstück 146 1985, black	LP $200
Meisterstück 146 1992, red (not shown)	LP $200
Meisterstück 149 1985, black	LP $325
Solitaire 1443 1985, gold-plated, grain guilloche	LP $650
Solitaire 1448 1985, sterling silver, stripe guilloche	LP $500

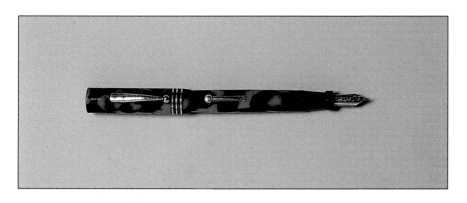

Morrison's

Morrison's Tourist ca. 1930, black and pearl	$150
Morrison's ca. 1925 Lady gold-plated, with loop	$55
Morrison's ca. 1925 Pencil, gold-plated	$35
Morrison's ca. 1925 gold-plated, wave guilloche	$90
Morrison's ca. 1925 gold-plated, smooth	$90
Morrison's ca. 1925 gold filled, wave guilloche	$12
Morrison's ca. 1930 black, wave guilloche	$35
Morrison's DBS ca. 1930 black, wave guilloche	$1.
Morrison's Tourist ca. 1930 black, cross guilloche	$35
Morrison's ca. 1930 black, smooth, anchor	$8
Morrison's Tourist ca. 1930, black	$1

Osmia (1919-1950)

Taken over by Faber-Castell in 1950
Faber-Castell (1761 to date)

J. Faber Pencil Case, ca. 1915, round, spiral pattern	$22
A. W. Faber Pencil Case, ca. 1906, flat version	$22
A. W. Faber Pen, ca. 1910, wood version	$22

In the firm's early years, hundreds of different models were made with decorations, in solid gold, etc.

Osmia pencil 165 ca. 1925, blue/red/white/green m.	$30
Osmia Brilliant pencil 659 ca. 1935	$22
blue/black marbled	
4-Color F.-Castell 33/75 1951, silver-plated	$18
07 Faber-Castell ballpoint 1957, black/gold filled cap	$8
202 Faber-Castell ballpoint 1957, black	$8

There were seven different barrel colors for the 07 ballpoint, worth $8 more.

In 1928 Osmia was taken over by Parker for a short time. For fountain pens, see the Parker price guide.
Progress and Super Progress pens were made in eight versions and four colors.

Osmia 52 ca. 1955, gray marbled	$35
Osmia 222 ca. 1945, gray/red/black marbled	$35
Osmia 93 Progress ca. 1935, red/black marbled	$35
Osmia 661 Faber-Castell ca. 1950	$35
red/black marbled	
Osmia ca. 1945, red/black marbled	$35
Osmia Brilliant 127 D ca. 1935, green striped	$55

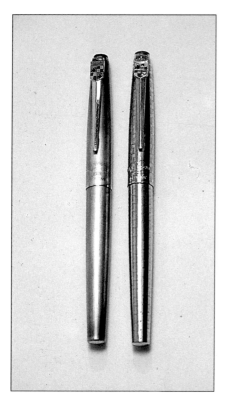

Osmia/Faber Castell

Osmia 72 ca. 1935	$22
black guilloche	
Osmia 74 ca. 1935	$30
black guilloche	
Osmia 74A ca. 1935	$35
black guilloche	
Osmia 72 Supra ca. 1935	$22
black smooth	
Osmia 13D ca. 1935	$30
black smooth	
Osmia 223 ca. 1935, dark gray	$30
Osmia/F.-C. Brilliant 03	$10
ca. 1955, gray	
Osmia/Faber-Castell 661	$22
ca. 1955, black	
Osmia/Faber-Castell 012	$30
ca. 1955, black	
Osmia/Faber-Castell 64	$35
ca. 1935, black	
Osmia/Faber-Castell 661	$18
ca. 1965, black	

Supra Luxus and Supra were available in ten versions and four colors.

A. W. Faber-Castell 5005	$70	**Castell 500 School Pen** 1974	$5
1972, 925 sterling silver		blue	
A. W. Faber-Castell 5002	$215	**Castell 500 School Pen** 1974	$5
1973, 585 gold		red	
A. W. Faber-Castell 5000	$285	**Castell 500 School Pen** 1974	$5
1972, 750 gold		green	
A. W. Faber-Castell 5001	$215	**Castell 500 School Pen** 1974	$5
1972, 585 gold		orange	
A. W. Faber-Castell 5003 Silgo 1972,		**Castell 500 School Pen** 1974	$5
925 with gold coating	$110	pink	
(not shown)			

Parker
(1888 to date)

Eyedropper No. 18 1900	$325-375
Red Ripple	
Eyedropper No. 24 1900	$350-425
Red Ripple	
Eyedropper No. 3 1898	$400-450
Red Ripple, conical	
Eyedropper No. 9 ca. 1900	$275-325
two gold-plated bands	
Eyedropper No. 21 ca. 1900	$300-350
two gold-plated bands	

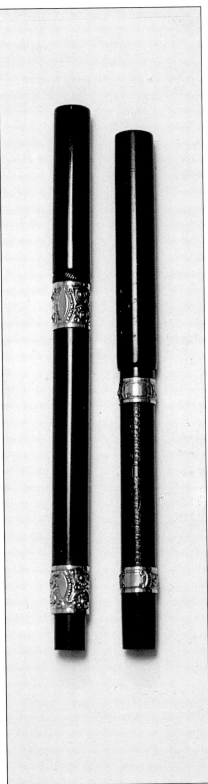

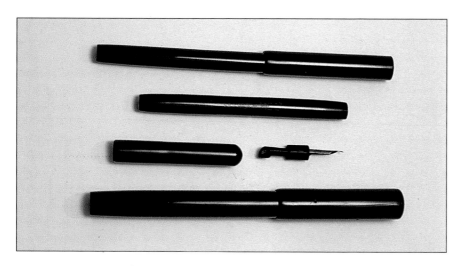

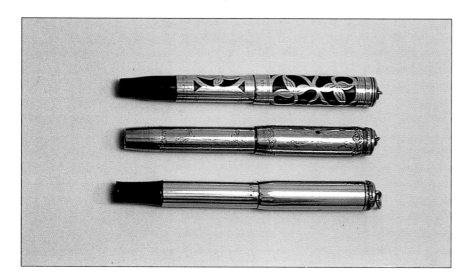

Jointless No. 018 1900 $225-3●
smooth black
Jointless No. 018 1900 $225-3●
smooth black
Jointless No. 026 1900 $400-5●
smooth black

Eyedroppers were filled by pulling out or
unscrewing the front end of the pen. In the
Jointless, only the point was pulled out.

Jack Knife 20 1916 $60-80
smooth black (not shown)
Jack Knife 20 1/2 1916 $60-80
black guilloche (not shown)
Jack Knife 24 1916 $135-1●
smooth black (not shown)
Jack Knife 25 1916 $275-2●
smooth black
Jack Knife 25 1/2 1916 $275-2●
black guilloche
Jack Knife 28 1916 $415-4●
smooth black (not shown)

Jack Knife 14 Filigree $500-6●
1918, sterling silver
Jack Knife Sterling 1918 $500-6●
floral design
Jack Knife gold filled 1918 $400-5●
smooth

Parker 160 1910 $700-800
gold-plated, filigree

Lucky Curve No. 1 1917 $55-65
smooth, Flat Top
Lucky Curve black 1917 $55-65
wave guilloche, Flat Top
Lucky Curve No. 22 1917 $90-110
smooth black, Flat Top
Lucky Curve No. 222 1917 $90-110
wave guilloche, Flat Top
Lucky Curve black 1917 $90-110
striped guilloche
Lucky Curve black 1917 $145-160
striped guilloche, one band

D. Q. Duofold Quality 1926 $145-160
black, with silver band
Parallel to the Duofold series was the D. Q.
series, a lower-priced alternative.

Streamline black pen	$50
1932, waved guilloche, ring	
Streamline black pen	$55
1932, waved guilloche, clip	
Streamline black pen	$70
1932, smooth, without bands	
Streamline black pen	$70
1932, waved guilloche, without bands	
Streamline black pen	$80
1932, waved guilloche, two bands	
Streamline black pen	$80
1932, smooth, two bands	
Duofold black 1927	$65
Lady Deluxe, ring, Flat Top	
Duofold black 1927	$55
Lady, ring, three bands, Flat Top	
Duofold black 1927	$55
Lady, clip, two bands	
Duofold black 1927	$90
Junior, one band, Flat Top	
Duofold black 1927	$90
Junior, two bands, Flat Top (not shown)	
Duofold black 1927 (?)	$530
Special, prototype, Flat Top	
Duofold black 1927	$200
Special, Flat Top, one band	
Duofold black 1927	$200
Special, Flat Top, two bands	
Duofold black 1927	$250
Senior, one band, Flat Top	
Duofold black 1927	$250
Senior, two bands, Flat Top	
Duofold black 1929	$45
Lady, ring, three bands, streamline (not shown)	
Duofold black 1929	$70
Lady, clip, two bands, streamline (not shown)	
Duofold black 1929	$80
Lady, clip, three bands, streamline	
Duofold black 1929	$90
Junior, two bands, streamline	
Duofold black 1929	$150
Special, two bands, streamline	
Duofold black 1929	$250
Senior, two bands, streamline	

Duo. Mandarin Yellow	$175	**Pencil** ca. 1915	$35-40
1927, Lady, ring, three bands, Flat Top		gold-plated	
Duo. Mandarin Yellow	$175		
1927, Lady, clip, Flat Top (not shown)		**Duofold Lapislazuli** 1927	$145
Duo. Mandarin Yellow	$250	Lady, clip, Flat Top	
1927, Junior, one band, Flat Top		**Duofold Lapislazuli** 1927	$145
Duo. Mandarin Yellow	$250	Lady, ring, two bands, Flat Top	
1927, Junior, two bands, Flat Top		**Duofold Lapislazuli** 1927	$145
(not shown)		Lady, ring, three bands, Flat Top	
Duo. Mandarin Yellow	$500	**Duofold Lapislazuli** 1927	$175
1927, Special, Flat Top (not shown)		Junior, one band, Flat Top	
Duo. Mandarin Yellow	$800-1000	**Duofold Lapislazuli** 1927	$175
1927, Senior, one band, Flat Top		Junior, two bands, Flat Top	
Duo. Mandarin Yellow	$800-1000	**Duofold Lapislazuli** 1927	$350-400
1928, Senior, two bands, Flat Top		Special, Flat Top	
(not shown)		**Duofold Lapislazuli** 1927	$600-700
Duo. Mandarin Yellow	$145	Senior, one band, Flat Top (not shown)	
1929, Lady, ring, three bands, streamline		**Duofold Lapislazuli** 1928	$600-700
Duo. Mandarin Yellow	$145	Senior, two bands, Flat Top	
1929, Lady, clip, two bands, streamline			
(not shown)			
Duo. Mandarin Yellow	$215		
1929, Junior, streamline (not shown)			
Duo. Mandarin Yellow	$425		
1929, Special, streamline (not shown)			
Duo. Mandarin Yellow	$700-900		
1929, Senior, one band, streamline			
(not shown)			
Duo. Mandarin Yellow	$700-900		
1929, Senior, two bands, streamline			
(not shown)			

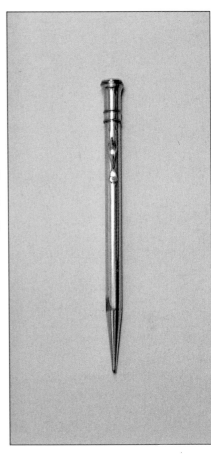

Duofold Lapislazuli 1929	$125	**Duofold Lapislazuli** 1929	$350	**Duofold green** 1926	$12

Duofold Lapislazuli 1929 $125
Lady, ring, streamline

Duofold Lapislazuli 1929 $125
Lady, clip, streamline

Duofold Lapislazuli 1929 $145
Junior, streamline (not shown)

Duofold Lapislazuli 1929 $350
Special, streamline

Duofold Lapislazuli 1929 $500-650
Senior, streamline

Duofold green 1926 $12
Lady, clip, Flat Top

Duofold green 1926 $12
Lady, ring, three bands, Flat Top

Duofold green 1926 $12
Lady de Luxe, one band

Duofold green 1926 $16
Junior, one band, Flat Top (not shown)

Duofold green 1926 $16
Junior, two bands, Flat Top

Duofold green 1926 $36
Special, Flat Top (not shown)

Duofold green 1926 $350-
Senior, one band, Flat Top

Duofold green 1926 $350-
Senior, two bands, Flat Top

Duofold green 1929 $11
Lady, ring, two bands, streamline

Duofold green 1929 $11
Lady, ring, three bands, streamline

Duofold green 1929 $11
Lady, ring, three bands, streamline

Duofold green 1929 $11
Lady, clip, three bands, streamline

Duofold green 1929 $14
Junior, streamline

Duofold green 1929 $28
Special, streamline

Duofold green 1929 $350-
Senior, streamline

Duofold orange 1927	$110
Lady de Luxe, ring, Flat Top	
Duofold orange 1927	$90
Lady, clip, three bands, Flat Top	
Duofold orange 1923	$215
Junior, hard rubber, Flat Top	
Duofold orange 1926	$125
Junior, one band, Flat Top	
Duofold orange 1927	$125
Junior, two bands, Flat Top	
Duofold orange 1927	$175
Special, Flat Top, one band	
Duofold orange 1927	$175
Special, Flat Top, two bands	
Duofold orange 1923	$350-400
Senior de Luxe, hard rubber	
Duofold orange 1927	$250
Senior, one band, Flat Top	
Duofold orange 1927	$250
Senior, two bands, Flat Top	
Duofold orange 1929	$70
Ring, three bands, streamline	
Duofold orange 1929	$70
Ring, three bands, streamline	
Duofold orange 1929	$70
Clip, three bands, streamline	
Duofold orange 1929	$110
Junior, two bands, streamline	
Duofold orange 1929	$145
Special, streamline	
Duofold orange 1929	$215
Senior, two bands, streamline	

Duofold Black and Pearl	$175
1928, Lady, ring, Flat Top	
Duofold Black and Pearl	$160
1929, Lady, streamline	
Duofold Black and Pearl	$285
1928, Junior, Flat Top	
Duofold Black and Pearl	$250
1929, Junior, streamline	
Duofold Black and Pearl	$200-500 (color important)
1928, Senior, Flat Top	

Duofold Black and Pearl	$200-500
1929, Senior, streamline	(color important)

The series was also called Duofold de Luxe.

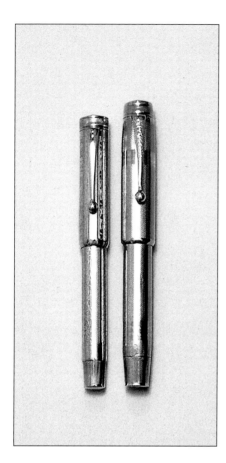

Duofold 14 Karat ca. 1925	$1600-2200
Lady, floral decorations	
Duofold 14 Karat ca. 1925	$2000-2500
Junior, grain guilloche	
Petite Pastel 1926	$100-145
olive with clip	
Petite Pastel 1926	$100-145
orange with clip	
Petite Pastel 1926	$100-145
green striped with clip (not shown)	
Petite Pastel 1926	$100-145
blue striped with clip (not shown)	
Petite Pastel 1926	$90-100
strawberry with ring	
Petite Pastel 1926	$90-100
blue with ring (not shown)	
Petite Pastel	$90-100
$125	
blue striped with ring (not shown)	
Petite Pastel 1926	$90-100
green striped with ring	
Petite Pastel 1926	$90-100
red striped with ring (not shown)	

Parker-Osmia, Duofold	$200	
1929, Lady, blue, three bands		
Parker-Osmia, Duofold	$150	Since Parker and Osmia were in joint production
1929, Junior, black, two bands		for only a short time, these pens with the Parker-
Parker-Osmia, Duofold	$250	Osmia name are found very rarely. They were
1929, Special, black, two bands		issued in all sizes and colors.

Duofold gold-plated 1925	$145
Lady, ring	
Duofold gold-plated 1925	$175
Lady, clip	
Duofold gold-plated 1925	$215
Lady, clip, floral decoration	
Duofold gold-plated 1920	$700-800
Junior, octagonal, stripes	
Duofold gold-plated 1920	$700-800
Junior, octagonal, grain guilloche	
Duofold Vest Pocket 1930	$1600-2200
18-karat white gold	
Duofold Vest Pocket 1930	$1600-2200
18-karat yellow gold	
Duofold Vest Pocket 1930	$200-300
Lapis lazuli (not shown)	
Duofold Vest Pocket 1930	$200-300
green (not shown)	
Duofold Vest Pocket 1930	$300-400
Mandarin yellow (not shown)	
Duofold Vest Pocket 1930	$145
Black (not shown)	
Duofold Vest Pocket 1930	$200-300
orange (not shown)	
Duofold Vest Pocket 1930	$200-250
Black and pearl (not shown)	

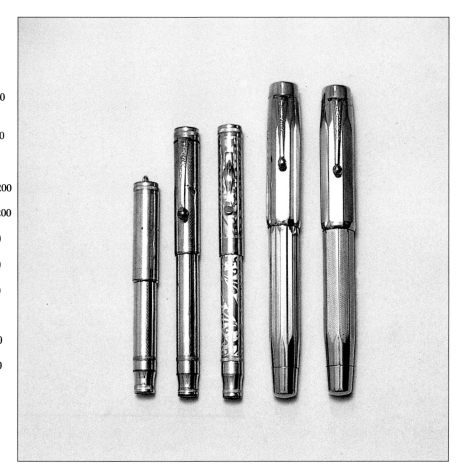

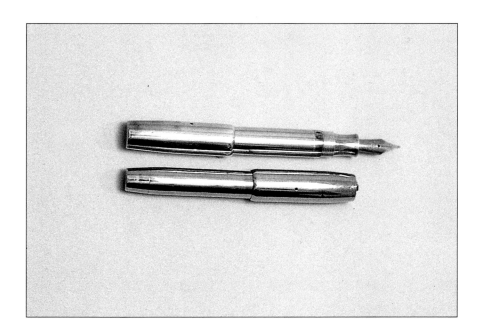

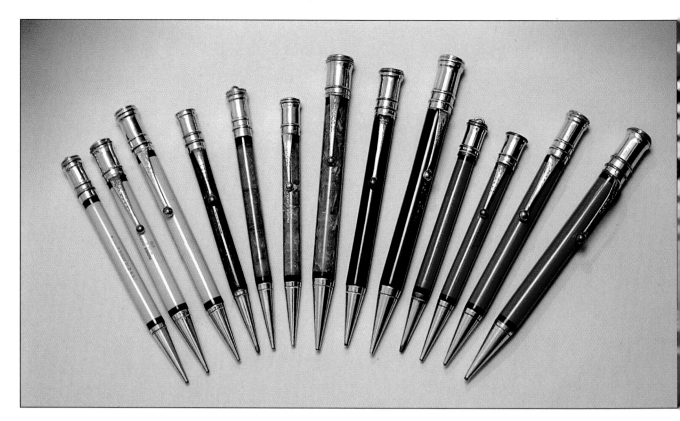

Mandarin Yellow pencil 1927 Lady, ring, Flat Top	$110	**Green pencil** 1926 Senior, Flat Top	$145	**Black and pearl pencil** 1928 Junior, Flat Top (not shown)	$125
Mandarin Yellow pencil 1927 Lady, clip, Flat Top	$110	**Black pencil** 1927 Lady, ring, Flat Top (not shown)	$55	**Black and pearl pencil** 1928 Senior, Flat Top (not shown)	$175
Mandarin Yellow pencil 1927 Junior, Flat Top	$145	**Black pencil** 1927 Lady, clip, Flat Top (not shown)	$55	**Green and pearl pencil** 1928 Lady, ring, Flat Top (not shown)	$90
Mandarin Yellow pencil 1927 Senior, Flat Top (not shown)	$250	**Black pencil** 1927 Junior, Flat Top	$70	**Green and pearl pencil** 1928 Lady, clip, Flat Top (not shown)	$90
Lapislazuli pencil 1927 Lady, ring, Flat Top (not shown)	$90	**Black pencil** 1927 Senior, Flat Top	$110	**Green and pearl pencil** 1928 Junior, Flat Top (not shown)	$125
Lapislazuli pencil 1927 Lady, clip, Flat Top	$90	**Orange pencil** 1927 Lady, ring, Flat Top	$55	**Green and pearl pencil** 1928 Senior, Flat Top (not shown)	$150
Lapislazuli pencil 1927 Junior, Flat Top (not shown)	$125	**Orange pencil** 1927 Lady, clip, Flat Top	$55		
Lapislazuli pencil 1927 Senior, Flat Top (not shown)	$175	**Orange pencil** 1925 Junior, Flat Top	$70		
Green pencil 1926 Lady, ring, Flat Top	$70	**Orange pencil** 1927 Senior, Flat Top	$110		
Green pencil 1926 Lady, clip, Flat Top	$70	**Black and pearl pencil** 1928 Lady, ring, Flat Top (not shown)	$90		
Green pencil 1926 Junior, Flat Top (not shown)	$110	**Black and pearl pencil** 1928 Lady, clip, Flat Top (not shown)	$90		

Mandarin Yellow pencil 1929, Lady, streamline (not shown)	$70
Mandarin Yellow pencil 1929, Junior, streamline (not shown)	$110
Mandarin Yellow pencil 1929, Senior, streamline (not shown)	$200-250
Lapislazuli pencil 1929 Lady, streamline	$55
Lapislazuli pencil 1929 Junior, streamline (not shown)	$70
Lapislazuli pencil 1929 Senior, streamline (not shown)	$145
Green pencil 1929 Lady, streamline	$55
Green pencil 1929 Junior, streamline (not shown)	$70
Green pencil 1929 Senior, streamline	$110
Black pencil 1929 Lady, streamline (not shown)	$40
Black pencil 1929 Junior, streamline	$70
Black pencil 1929 Senior, streamline (not shown)	$90
Orange pencil 1929 Lady, streamline (not shown)	$45
Orange pencil 1929 Junior, streamline (not shown)	$70
Orange pencil 1929 Senior, streamline	$90
Black and pearl pencil 1929 Lady, streamline (not shown)	$70
Black and pearl pencil 1929 Junior, streamline (not shown)	$110
Black and pearl pencil 1929 Senior, streamline	$175
Green and pearl pencil 1929 Lady, streamline (not shown)	$70
Green and pearl pencil 1929 Junior, streamline (not shown)	$110
Green and pearl pencil 1929 Senior, streamline (not shown)	$175

Duofold sea green pearl 1930, Lady, with clip	$110
Duofold sea green pearl 1930, Lady, with ring (not shown)	$110
Duofold sea gren pearl 1930, Junior	$145
Duofold sea green pearl 1930, Special	$250
Duofold sea green pearl 1930, pencil	$90
Duofold sea green pearl 1930, Senior	$350-450
Duofold sea green pearl 1930, pencil (not shown)	$145

Duofold burgundy 1931 Lady, with clip	$110	**True blue** 1929 Lady, ring, Flat Top	$110
Duofold burgundy 1931 Lady, with ring	$110	**True blue** 1929 Lady, clip, streamline	$110
Duofold burgundy 1931 Junior (not shown)	$145	**True blue pencil** 1929 Flat Top	$55
Duofold burgundy 1931 Special (not shown)	$250	**True blue** 1929 Juniorette, streamline	$145
Duofold burgundy 1931 Pencil	$90		
Duofold burgundy 1931 Senior	$360		
Duofold burgundy 1931 Pencil	$145		

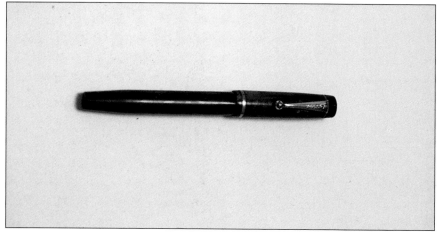

Depression 1935 $90-300 (depends on color)
gold/brown marbled
In the thirties, several low-priced models were
produced in non-standard Parker colors.

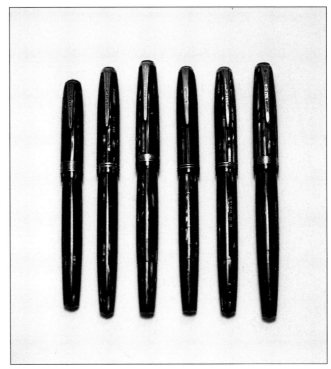

Duofold green and pearl 1932 $215
light green/black marbled
Duofold Geometric ca. 1940,
light green/black $215
Duofold Geometric ca. 1940, gold/black $215
Duofold blue ca. 1940, marbled $320

Duofold green striped ca. 1940, small version $125-145
Duofold green striped ca. 1940 medium version $150-175
Duofold green striped ca. 1940, large version $215
Duofold red striped ca. 1940 $125-145
small version (not shown)
Duofold red striped ca. 1940, medium version $150-175
Duofold red striped ca. 1940 $215
large version (not shown)
Duofold blue striped ca. 1940 $125-160
small version (not shown)
Duofold blue striped ca. 1940, medium version $125-175
Duofold blue striped ca. 1940, large version $175-250
Green striped pencil ca. 1940, one wide band (not shown) $45-60
Green striped pencil ca. 1940, two bands (not shown) $45-60
Green striped pencil ca. 1940, 3 bands (not shown) $45-60
Red striped pencil ca. 1940, 1 wide band $45-60
(not shown)
Red striped pencil ca. 1940, two bands $45-60
Red striped pencil ca. 1940, three bands (not shown) $45-60
Blue striped pencil ca. 1940, one wide band $45-60
Blue striped pencil ca. 1940, two bands (not shown) $45-60
Blue striped pencil ca. 1940, three bands $45-60

Vacumatic Standard 1933 gold	$100-135	**Vacumatic Gold Web** 1934	$175-200
Vacumatic Standard 1933 silver	$90-125	**Vacumatic Shadow Wave** 1938, gray striped	$110
Vacumatic Standard 1933 red	$120-175	**Vacumatic Shadow Wave** 1938, Junior, gray striped (not shown)	$145
Vacumatic Standard 1933 green	$120-175	**Vacumatic Shadow Wave** 1938, Junior, red striped (not shown)	$145
Vacumatic Standard 1933 blue (not shown)	$100-135	**Vacumatic Shadow Wave** 1938, Junior, green striped	$145
Vacumatic Standard 1933 black	$70-90	**Vacumatic Shadow Wave** 1938 1938, Junior, gold striped (not shown)	$145
Vacumatic Oversize 1933 gold (not shown)	$285		
Vacumatic Oversize 1933 silver	$285		
Vacumatic Oversize 1933 red (not shown)	$425		
Vacumatic Oversize 1933 green (not shown)	$425		
Vacumatic Oversize 1933 green (not shown)	$425		
Vacumatic Oversize 1933 blue (not shown)	$400-500		
Vacumatic Oversize 1933 black (not shown)	$285		

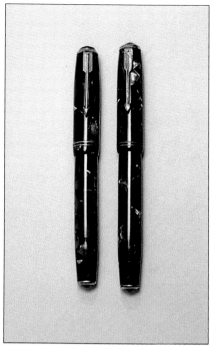

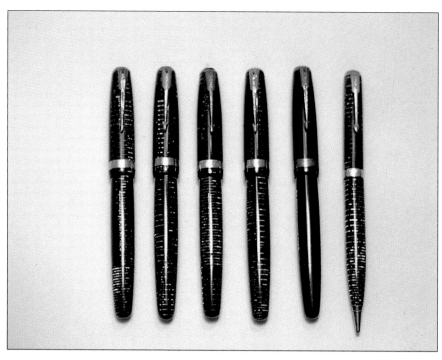

Vacumatic Junior 1934 gray marbled, stainless steel clip	$180
Vacumatic Junior 1934 gray marbled, gold-plated clip	$180
Vacumatic Major 1939 gold	$145
Vacumatic Major 1939 silver	$145
Vacumatic Major 1939 red (not shown)	$180
Vacumatic Major 1939 green	$180
Vacumatic Major 1939 blue	$215
Vacumatic Major 1939 black	$145
Vacumatic Major pencil 1939 gold	$90
Vacumatic Major pencil 1939 silver (not shown)	$90
Vacumatic Major pencil 1939 red (not shown)	$110
Vacumatic Major pencil 1939 green (not shown)	$110
Vacumatic Major pencil 1939 blue (not shown)	$145
Vacumatic Major pencil 1939 black (not shown)	$90

Vacumatic Debutante 1939 gold	$90
Vacumatic Debutante 1939 silver	$90
Vacumatic Debutante 1939 red (not shown)	$110
Vacumatic Debutante 1939 green	$110
Vacumatic Debutante 1939 blue (not shown)	$125
Vacumatic Debutante 1939 black	$60-80
Vacumatic Debutante pencil 1939, gold (not shown)	$35-45
Vacumatic Debutante 1939, silver (not shown)	$50

Vacumatic Debutante pencil 1939, red (not shown)	$35-45
Vacumatic Debutante pencil 1939, green (not shown)	$35-45
Vacumatic Debutante pencil 1939, blue (not shown)	$35-45
Vacumatic Debutante pencil 1939, black (not shown)	$25-35

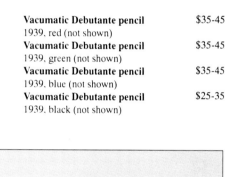

Vacumatic Junior 1939, gold	$85-120
Vacumatic Junior 1939, silver	$75-100
Vacumatic Junior 1939, red (not shown)	$85-120
Vacumatic Junior 1939, green	$85-120
Vacumatic Junior 1939, blue	$85-120
Vacumatic Junior 1939, black	$75-100
Vacumatic Junior pencil 1939, gold (not shown)	$30-40
Vacumatic Junior pencil 1939, silver (not shown)	$30-40
Vacumatic Junior pencil 1939, red (not shown)	$30-40
Vacumatic Junior pencil 1939, green (not shown)	$30-40
Vacumatic Junior pencil 1939, blue	$35-45
Vacumatic junior pencil 1939, black (not shown)	$30-40

Vacumatics were also made in other versions, but the prices are always the same on the basis of the size.

Challenger Slender 1939, black	$60
Challenger pencil 1939, black (not shown)	$25-35
Challenger Slender 1939, green marbled	$70
Challenger pencil 1939, green marbled	$25-35
Challenger Slender 1939, red marbled	$70
Challenger pencil 1939, red marbled (not shown)	$25-35
Challenger Slender 1939, gray marbled (not shown)	$50
Challenger pencil 1939, gray marbled (not shown)	$20-30
Challenger Standard 1939, black (not shown)	$90
Challenger Standard 1939, green marbled (not shown)	$110
Challenger Standard 1939, red marbled	$110
Challenger Standard 1939, gray marbled	$110
Royal Challenger 1939 golden brown marbled, Slender (not shown)	$175-225
Royal Challenger pencil 1939, golden brown marbled	$50-75
Royal Challenger 1939 maroon marbled, Slender (not shown)	$175-225
Royal Challenger pencil 1939 maroon marbled (not shown)	$50-75
Royal challenger 1939 gray marbled, Slender (not shown)	$165-180
Royal Challenger pencil 1939 gray marbled (not shown)	$40-50
Royal Challenger 1939, golden brown, Standard	$200-225
Royal Challenger 1939 maroon, Standard (not shown)	$200-225
Royal Challenger 1939 gray marbled, Standard (not shown)	$175-200
Deluxe Challenger 1939 gray marbled, Standard	$60-80

The Deluxe series was also made in two sizes (Slender and Standard), in black, gray marbled, green marbled and gray marbled colors. For prices, see Royal challenger.

Moderne pen ca. 1932, black	$55
Moderne pencil ca. 1932, black	$30
Moderne pen ca. 1932, gold-green marbled	$100-175
Moderne pencil ca. 1932	$55
gold-green marbled (not shown)	
Moderne pen ca. 1932, brown-blue marbled	$100-175
Moderne pencil ca. 1932	$55
brown-blue marbled (not shown)	
Moderne pen ca. 1932, beige marbled	$100-175
Moderne pencil ca. 1932	$55
beige marbled (not shown)	
Moderne pen with ring ca. 1932	$145
green-gold marbled	
Premiere ca. 1932, black	$70-90
Premiere ca. 1932, mahogany	$125-200
Premiere ca. 1932, blue marbled	$125-200
Premiere ca. 1932, gray/red marbled	$125-200
Parkette de Luxe ca. 1935, black	$50
Parkette de Luxe ca. 1935, gray marbled	$65-75
Parkette de Luxe ca. 1935, red marbled	$65-75
Parkette de Luxe ca. 1935, green marbled	$65-75

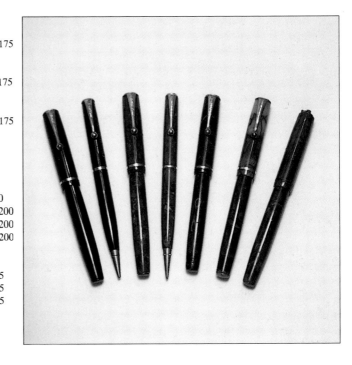

In the thirties, the Parkette was a low-priced Parker series which was produced in various versions in various countries. In addition, it is the only Parker series to be built with a lever mechanism.

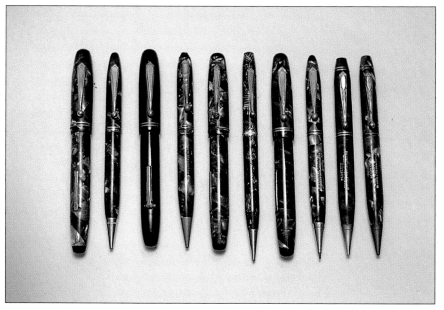 

Parkette pen ca. 1935 green marbled	$50	**Parkette pencil** ca. 1935 red striped	$30	**Parkette Zephyr** 1939 gray marbled	$50-70
Parkette pencil ca. 1935 green marbled	$25	**Parkette pen** ca. 1935 gray-red marbled	$50	**Parkette Zephyr** 1939 gold marbled	$50-70
Parkette pen ca. 1935 black	$35	**Parkette pencil** ca. 1935 gray-red marbled	$25	**Parkette Zephyr** 1939 blue marbled	$50-70
Parkette pencil ca. 1935 black (not shown)	$15	**Parkette pen** ca. 1935 red marbled (not shown)	$75	**Parkette Zephyr** 1939 black (not shown)	$35-50
Parkette pen ca. 1935 green-brown marbled (not shown)	$50	**Parkette pencil** ca. 1935 red marbled	$30	**Parkette Zephyr** 1939 in all four colors (not shown)	$35
Parkette pencil ca. 1935 green-brown marbled	$25	**Parkette pen** ca. 1935 green marbled (not shown)	$75		
Parkette pen ca. 1935 red marbled	$75	**Parkette pencil** ca. 1935 green marbled	$30		
Parkette pencil ca. 1935 red marbled (not shown)	$30				
Parkette pen ca. 1935 red striped (not shown)	$65				

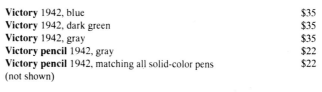

Televisor ca. 1945, green striped, small	$90
Televisor ca. 1945, red striped, small	$90
(not shown)	
Televisor ca. 1945, gray striped, small	$90
(not shown)	
Televisor ca. 1945, black, small	$70
(not shown)	
Televisor ca. 1945, green striped, large	$145
Televisor ca. 1945, red striped, large	$145
Televisor ca. 1945, gray striped, large	$145
Televisor ca. 1945, black, large	$110
Televisor pencil ca. 1945, green striped	$35
(not shown)	
Televisor pencil ca. 1945, red striped (not shown)	$35
Televisor pencil ca. 1945, gray striped	$35
(not shown)	
Televisor pencil ca. 1945, black	$20
Victory 1935, black	$55
Victory 1935, red marbled	$70
Victory 1935, green marbled	$70
Victory Candy Stripe 1935, red striped	$110
Victory Candy Stripe 1935, green striped	$110
Victory Candy Stripe 1935, brown striped	$110
Victory Candy Stripe 1935, gray striped	$145
Victory Geometric 1942, green/black marbled	$178
Victory 1942, brown	$35

Victory 1942, blue	$35
Victory 1942, dark green	$35
Victory 1942, gray	$35
Victory pencil 1942, gray	$22
Victory pencil 1942, matching all solid-color pens	$22
(not shown)	

VS 1947 black/gold	$90
VS 1947 rust red/stainless steel	$55
VS 1947 blue/stainless steel	$55
VS 1947 maroon/gold-plated	$70
VS 1947 blue/gold-plated	$70
VS 1947 black/gold-plated	$70
VS (Prototype?) 1947 (?) aluminum	$360

51 Vacumatic System 1941 black/sterling silver cap	$145
51 Vacumatic System 1941 black/gold-plated	$110
51 Vacumatic System 1941 black/gold-plated	$90
51 Vacumatic System 1941 turquoise/gold-plated	$110
51 Vacumatic System 1941 black/stainless steel	$70
51 Pencil 1941 black/stainless steel	$25
51 Vacumatic System 1941 black/stainless steel	$70

These types were produced in various colors.

51 Aerometric 1948 black/18-karat gold cap	$900-1050
51 Aerometric 1948 9-karat gold	$360
51 Aerometric 1948 18-karat gold	$710

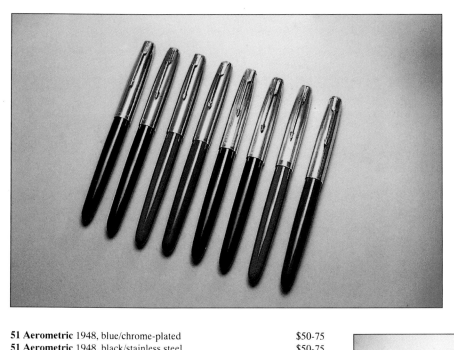

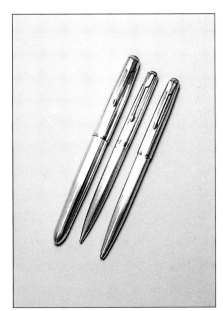

51 **Aerometric** 1948, blue/chrome-plated $50-75
51 **Aerometric** 1948, black/stainless steel $50-75
51 **Aerometric** 1948, light red/stainless steel $50-75
51 **Aerometric** 1948, gray/stainless steel $50-75
51 **Aerometric** 1948, dark red/gold-plated $60-85
51 **Aerometric** 1948, black/gold-plated $60-85
51 **Aerometric** 1948, light red/gold-plated $60-85
51 **Aerometric** 1948, gray/gold-plated $60-85
There are also many different colors of the later 51 series,
all of which can be evaluated similarly.

51 **Aeromatic pen** 1949, gold-plated $225
51 **Pencil** 1949, gold-plated $75
51 **Ballpoint** 1954, gold-plated $100

51 **Pencil** 1948, blue/chrome-plated $20-30
51 **Pencil** 1948, gray/chrome-plated $20-30
51 **Pencil** 1948, blue/stainless steel $20-30
51 **Pencil** 1948, light brown/stainless steel $20-30
51 **Pencil** 1948, turquoise/stainless steel $20-30
51 **Pencil** 1948, maroon/stainless steel $20-30
51 **Pencil** 1948, black/gold-plated $20-30
51 **Pencil** 1948, light brown/gold-plated $20-30
51 **Pencil** 1948, maroon/gold-plated $20-30
51 **Pencil** (Mail Coach) 1948 $110
Mexican model

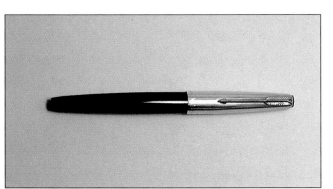

51 Vacumatic transparent 1941, display model	$175-200
51 Aerometric transparent 1948, display model	$145
45 transparent 1960, display model	$70
65 transparent 1967, display model	$70
Duofold 1946, maroon	$55
Duofold 1946, rust red	$70
Duofold 1946, black	$55
Duofold 1946, black	$55
Duofold 1946, dark brown	$55
Slimfold 1962, red	$45
Slimfold 1962, black	$45
Slimfold 1962, green	$45
Slimfold 1962, blue	$45
Duofold 1953, red	$60
Duofold 1953, black	$60
Duofold 1953, green	$60
Duofold 1953, blue (not shown)	$60
Senior Duofold 1954, red (not shown)	$110
Senior Duofold 1954, black	$110
Maxima Duofold 1958, green	$110
Maxima Duofold 1958, blue (not shown)	$110
VP 1962, black/gold	$110

17 Lady 1964	$35
black	
17 Lady 1964	$35
red (not shown)	
17 Lady 1964	$35
blue	
17 Lady 1964	$35
green (not shown)	
17 Lady 1964	$35
black/chrome-plated	
17 1964	$35
black, covered point	
17 1964	$35
red, covered point	
17 1964	$35
blue, covered point	
17 1964	$35
green, covered point	
17 1964	$45
black, chrome-plateD	
17 1964	$70
blue, gold-plated	
17 1964	$55
black, open point	
17 1964	$55
red, open point (not shown)	
17 1964	$55
blue, open point (not shown)	
17 1964	$55
green, open point	

Liquid Lead (for 51) 1955	$5-12
maroon/chrome-plated	
Liquid Lead (for 61) 1955	$5-12
red/stainless steel, gold clip	
Liquid Lead (for 61) 1955	$5-12
gray/gold-plated, Heirloom	
Liquid Lead (for 21) 1955	$5-12
blue/stainless steel	
Liquid Lead (for 21) 1955	$5-12
green/stainless steel	
Liquid Lead (for Jotter)	$5-12
ca. 1960, black/stainless steel	
Liquid Lead (for Jotter)	$5-12
ca. 1960, gray/stainless steel	

Liquid Lead was a pencil with liquid lead and
was filled with cartridges similar to those of
ballpoint pens.

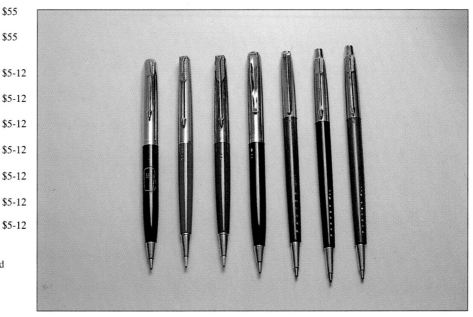

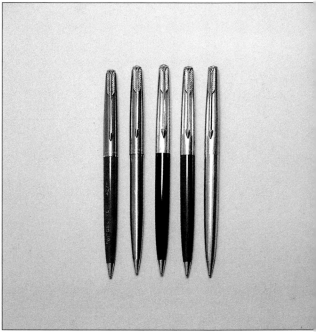

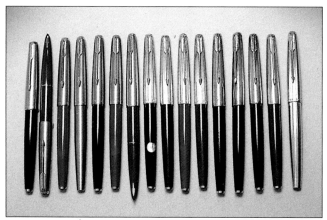

Jotter ballpoint 1954	$75	
green, first Parker ballpoint		
Jotter ballpoint 1954	$75	
red, first Parker ballpoint		
Window Jotter ballpoint 1969	$35	
open field for name etc.		
Jotter Demonstrator pencil	$50	
1969, display model		
61 Classic 1958	$70	
black/stainless steel		
61 Classic 1958	$70	
gray/stainless steel		
61 Classic 1958	$70	
turquoise/stainless steel		

61 Flighter 1958	$90
stainless steel	
61 de Luxe 1958	$90
black/stainless steel, gold clip	
61 de Luxe 1958	$90
turquoise/stainless steel, gold clip	
61 de Luxe 1958	$90
red/stainless steel, gold clip	
61 custom 1958	$70
black/gold-plated	
61 Custom 1958	$90
green/gold-plated	
61 Custom 1958	$90
turquoise/gold-plated	

61 Custom 1958	$
red/gold-plated	
61 Legacy 1958	$
black/nickel-silver-plated	
61 Heritage 1958	$
black/gold-plated	
61 Heirloom 1958	$
black/gold-plated	
61 Heirloom 1958	$
red/gold-plated	
61 Insignia 1958	$
gold-plated	
61 de Luxe pencil 1958	$
turquoise/stainless steel, gold clip	
61 Flighter pencil 1958	$
stainless steel, gold clip	
61 Custom pencil 1958	$
black, gold-plated	
61 Custom pencil 1958	$
gray, gold-plated	
61 Insignia pencil 1958	$
gray, gold-plated	
61 Insignia pencil 1958	$
gold-plated	

All 61's existed with the following barrel color: black, green, blue, red and turquoise. Later the capillary system was replaced by the normal cartridge system.

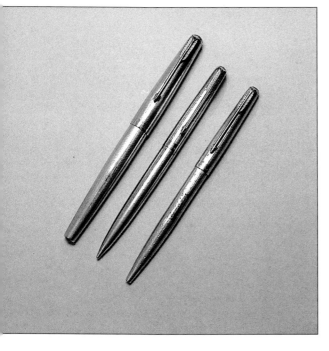

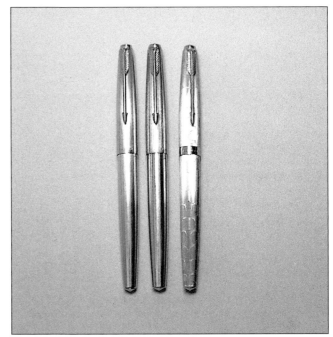

61 Waterdrop pen ca. 1970 $285
9-karat gold
61 Waterdrop pencil ca. 1970 $145
9-karat gold
61 Waterdrop ballpoint ca. 1970 $145
9-karat gold
61 Waterdrop pen ca. 1970 $530
18-karat gold (not shown)
61 Waterdrop pencil ca. 1970 $215
18-karat gold (not shown)
61 Waterdrop ballpoint ca. 1970 $215
18-karat gold (not shown)

61 Custom Insignia 1969 $145
gold-plated, fine stripes
61 Custom Insignia 1969 $145
gold-plated, wide stripes
61 Stratus 1976 $215
gold-plated, stripes, pattern

65 Classic 1967 $55
gray/stainless steel
65 Classic 1967 $55
black/stainless steel
65 Classic de Luxe (?) 1969 $55
black/stainless steel, gold clip
65 Flighter 1971 $55
stainless steel
65 Flighter de Luxe 1971 $60
stainless steel, gold clip
65 Custom 1967 $60
black/gold-plated

65 Custom 1967 $60
turquoise/gold-plated
65 Insignia 1967 $90
gold-plated
65 Presidential 1967 $425
14-karat gold
65 Presidential 1967 $570
18-karat gold (not shown)

The 65 series was likewise available with black, gray, blue,
turquoise and red barrel colors.

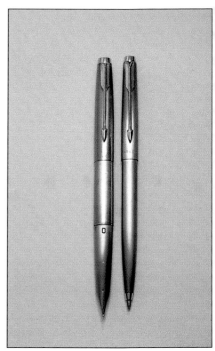

45 School Filler 1960	$5
black plastic	
45 School Filler 1960	$5
red plastic	
45 Standard 1960	$10
gray plastic	
45 Standard 1960	$10
green plastic	
45 Flighter 1960	$25-30
stainless steel	
45 Harlequin 1980	$55-80
stainless steel with pattern	
45 Harlequin 1980	$55-80
stainless steel with pattern	
45 Custom 1960	$35-50
black/rolled gold	
45 Coronet Flighter 1971	$20
black/stainless steel/gold-plated clip	
45 Coronet Flighter 1971	$20
blue/stainless steel/gold-plated clip	
45 Coronet 1969	$35
light blue dural	
45 Coronet 1969	$35
red dural	
45 Insignia 1960	$70
rolled gold	
45 Presidential 1967	$360
14-karat gold	

The 45 series was made with blue, black, red,
green, orange, yellow, turquoise and gray barrel
colors. The Insignia was made fully gold-plated
and with a black or blue end piece.

T-1 pen 1970	$350-425
titanium	
T-1 pencil 1970	$145
titanium	
T-1 ballpoint 1970	$175-225
titanium (not shown)	
T-1 roller ball 1970	$145
titanium (not shown)	

This series was produced for only about six
months and was then dropped on account of its
cost. The occasion of the models was the landing
on the moon!

5 Sterling 1967 erling silver, checkered	$80-125
5 Grain d'orge 1970 old-plated, grain guilloched	$110
5 Fileté 1970 old-plated, stripe guilloched	$110
5 Perlé 1970 old-plated/pearl guilloched	$110
5 Gaudron 1971 ver-plated/striped	$70
5 Ecossais 1971 ver-plated/plaid pattern	$110
5 Custom 1972 ack/gold-plated	$70
5 Jaspis 1978 range-painted	$110
5 Lapislazuli 1978 ue-painted	$110
5 Malachite 1978 reen-painted	$110
5 Thuja 1978 rown-painted	$70

ver the years, many different guilloched
atterns and painted versions were added.
he ballpoint pens, pencils and rollers can be
valuated at $35 to $50 apiece.

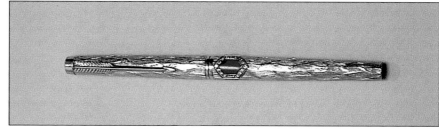

0 (Model for Boucheron) ca. 1980, 0 white-gold with diamonds and is lazuli	$1050

0 Flighter 1978 inless steel	$70
0 Painted 1981 e-painted	$70
0 Painted 1981 l-painted	$70
0 Painted 1981 ange-painted	$90
0 Painted 1981 uja (brown)-painted	$90
0 Place Vendome 1981 ver-plated	$110
0 Place Vendome 1981 d-plated	$110

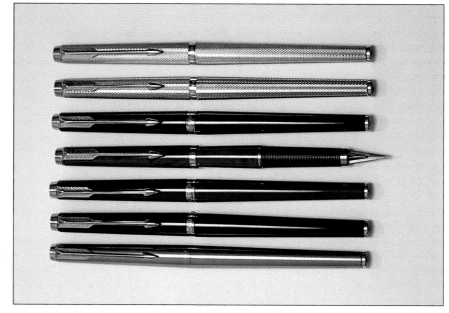

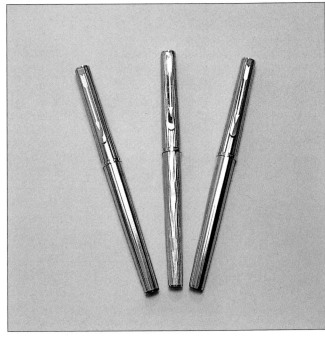

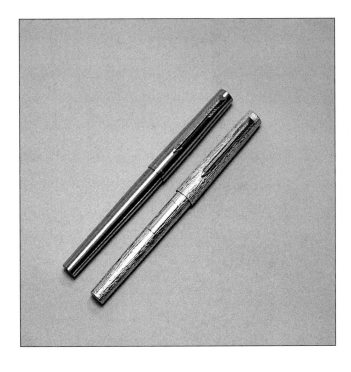

50 Flighter pen 1982	$35
stainless steel, gold clip	
50 Flighter ballpoint 1982	$25
stainless steel, gold clip	
50 Brown pen 1982	$55
brown epoxy	
50 Brown ballpoint 1982	$35
brown epoxy	
50 Black pen 1982	$45
black epoxy	
50 Black ballpoint 1982	$30
black epoxy	
50 Gold filled pen 1982	$110
gold-plated	
50 Gold filled ballpoint 1982	$55
gold-plated	
85 1981	$145
silver-plated	
85 1981	$215
sterling silver	
85 1981	$180
gold-plated	
This series was in production for only one year!	
105 ca. 1980	$145
stainless steel	
105 ca. 1980	$215
gold-plated	

Premier China Laque 1985	$145
Chinese lacquer/gold dust	
Premier gold plate/lacquer	$145
1985, gold-plated/lacquer stripes	
95 Laque ca. 1990	$70
turquoise, export model	
Arrow gold-plated 1982	$55
gold-plated	
Sonnet Fougere 1993	LP $370
sterling silver	
Sonnet Athenes 1993	LP $320
gold-plated/lacquer stripes	
Sonnet gold-plated	LP $185
1993, gold-plated	
Sonnet Laque 1993	LP $160
lacquered in red	
Duofold Onyx 1988	$215
black	
Duofold Sapphire 1988	$215
blue	
Duofold Ruby 1988	$215
red	
Duofold Jade (green) 1988	$360
only for American Express	

The series was made in two sizes;
deduct $35 for the values
of the smaller types.

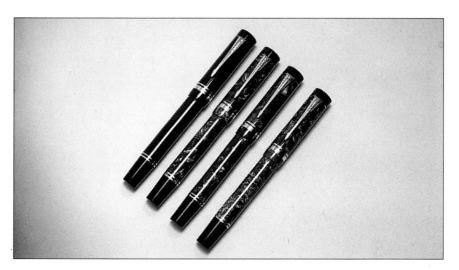

Duofold Onyx 1990	LP $200
black	
Duofold Sapphire 1990	LP $200
blue	
Duofold Ruby 1990	LP $200
red	
Duofold Jade 1991	LP $200
green	
Duofold de Luxe 1991	LP $200
orange	
Duofold de Luxe Opal	LP $250
1992, white/black marbled	
Duofold de Luxe 1992	LP $200
sterling silver	
Duofold de Luxe 1992	LP $180
gold-plated	
Duofold de Luxe	LP $13,475
1992, 18-karat gold (not shown)	

This series differs from the former in that the
decorative rings were made more rounded and
the pen was equipped with an 18-karat gold
point. There are also two sizes available. The
difference in value is $70.

Pelikan
(1838 to date)

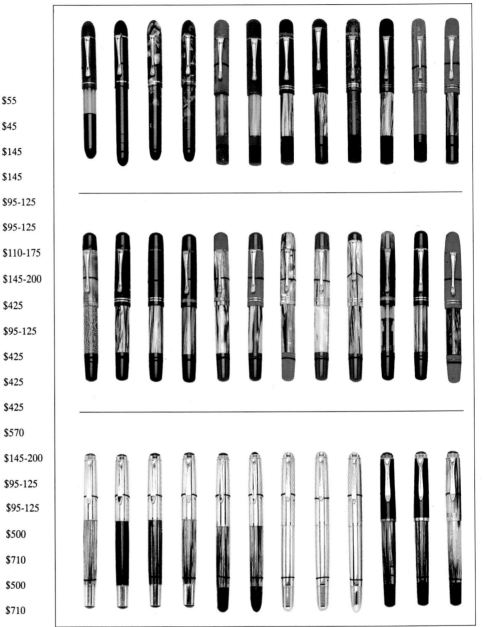

Rappen 1932	$55
black, transparent	
Ibis 1932	$45
black	
Ibis 1936	$145
gray marbled	
Ibis 1936	$145
brown marbled	
100 1929	$95-125
hard rubber, green marbled	
100 1929	$95-125
green marbled	
100 1929	$110-175
gray marbled	
100 1929	$145-200
gray marbled	
100 1929	$425
blue marbled	
100 1929	$95-125
green marbled	
100 1929	$425
orange	
100 1929	$425
orange marbled	
100 1929	$425
green marbled	
100 1929	$570
lizardskin	
100 1929	$145-200
brown marbled	
100 1929	$95-125
green marbled	
100 1929	$95-125
black	
100 Gold 1930	$500
14-karat gold band	
101 Gold 1930	$710
14-karat gold band and cap	
100 Weissgold 1931	$500
14-karat white-gold band	
101 Weissgold 1931	$710
14-karat white-gold band and cap	
100 Toledo 1934	$850-1000
24-karat gold decoration	
100 N 1937	$75-100
green marbled	
100 N 1937	$75-100
green marbled	
100 N 1937	$85-110
black	
100 N 1937	$570
lizardskin	

100 N 1937	$110-135	**100 N** 1937	$285-350
gray marbled		mother-of-pearl	
100 N 1937	$110-135	**100 N** 1937	$285-350
gray marbled		mother-of-pearl	
100 N 1939	$110-135	**100 N** 1937	$250-350
green marbled (clip missing)		mother-of-pearl	
100 N 1939	$145-175	**100 N** 1939	$215-300
tortoiseshell		transparent	
100 N 1939	$250	**100 N** 1937	$75-100
tortoiseshell		green marbled	

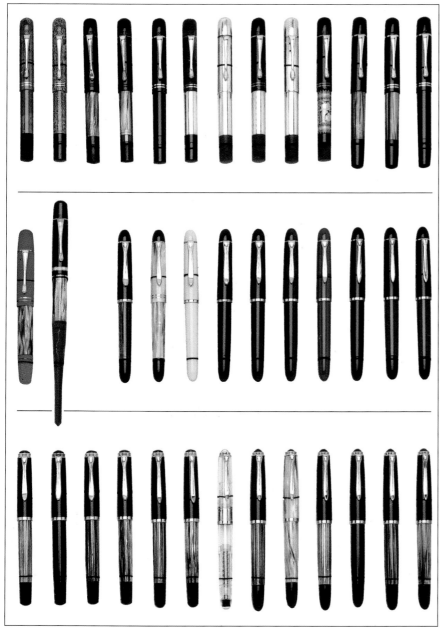

140 1952		$70
black, chrome-plated		
120 1955		$55
black-green		
120 1955		$55
black-green		
500 1950		$215
tortoiseshell-doubleé		
500 1950		$250
black-doubleé		
500 1950		$250
black-doubleé		
500 1950		$215
tortoiseshell-doubleé		
500N 1956		$215
tortoiseshell-doubleé		
500NN 1956		$250
tortoiseshell-doubleé		
520 1955		$285
rolled gold-doubleé		
520N 1955		$285
rolled gold-doubleé		
520 NN 1955		$320
rolled gold-doubleé		
400 1950		$70
green marbled		
400 1950		$70
green marbled		
400 1950		$285
mother-of-pearl		
400 1950		$215
gray marbled		
400 1950		$125
black		
400 1950		$70
green striped		
400 1950		$70
brown striped		
400 N 1955		$70
green striped		
400 N 1955		$70
brown striped		
400 NN 1956		$360
transparent		
400 NN 1956		$90
green striped		
400 NN 1956		$285
mother-of-pearl		
400 NN 1956		$180
gray striped		
400 NN 1956		$145
black		
400 NN 1956		$90
green striped		
400 NN 1956		$90
brown striped		

(The listings refer to the pens as shown straight across both pages.)

100 N 1937	$250	**140** 1952		$215
tortoiseshell		white		
100 N 1937	$250	**140** 1952		$55
tortoiseshell		black, gold filled decorations		
100 N 1939	$145	**140** 1952		$110
green marbled		dark green		
140 1952	$75-100	**140** 1952		$110
green striped		dark blue		
140 1952	$250-300	**140** 1952		$110
mother-of-pearl		maroon		

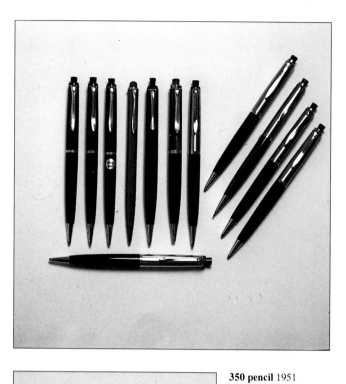

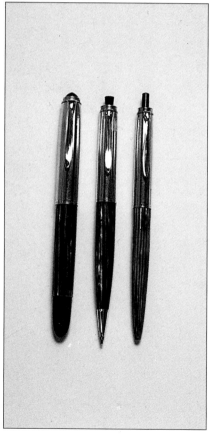

350 pencil 1951 green	$35
350 pencil 1951 dark blue	$45
350 pencil 1951 black	$35
350 pencil 1951 black/green (not shown)	$35
50F pencil 1953 light green	$35
50F pencil 1953 black (not shown)	$35
50F pencil 1953 wine-red (not shown)	$35
50F pencil 1953 light blue (not shown)	$35
50F pencil 1953 brown	$35
50F pencil 1953 gray (not shown)	$35
250 pencil 1951 black	$35
250 pencil 1951 black/green (not shown)	$35
450 pencil 1955 black (not shown)	$45
450 pencil 1955 black/green	$45
450 pencil 1955 tortoiseshell/brown (not shown)	$45
D15 pencil 1962 blue/stainless steel	$20

550 pencil ca. 1965 green/stainless steel	$20
550 pencil ca. 1965 blue/stainless steel (not shown)	$20
550 pencil ca. 1965 gray/stainless steel	$20
550 pencil ca. 1965 red/stainless steel	$20
550 pencil ca. 1965 black/stainless steel	$20
D25 pencil 1962 blue/gold-plated	$35
P1 S 1959 red/stainless steel cap	$55
P1 S 1959 gray/stainless steel cap	$55
P1 S 1959 black/stainless steel cap (not shown)	$55
P1 S 1959 green/stainless steel cap (not shown)	$55
P1 RG 1959 red/gold-plated cap	$70
P1 RG 1959 gray/gold-plated cap	$70
P1 RG 1959 black/gold filled cap (not shown)	$70
P1 RG 1959 green/gold-plated cap (not shown)	$70

500 NN pen 1956, tortoiseshell, gold-plated
550 pencil 1951,
tortoiseshell, gold-plated $360 set
555 ballpoint (?) ca. 1956, tortoiseshell, gold-plated

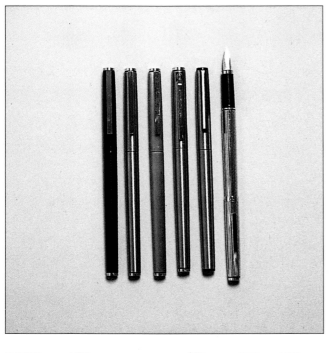

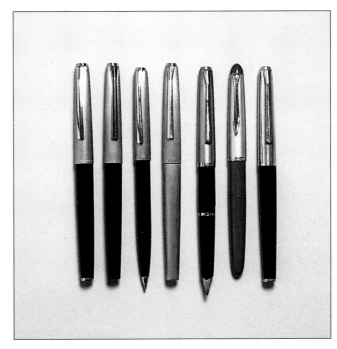

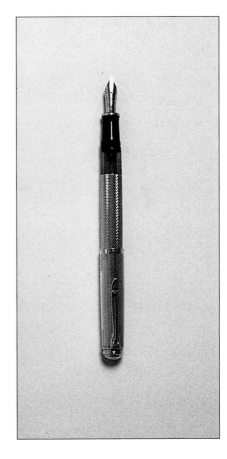

P 620 Signum 1984	$20	**P 30 pen** 1966	$22
black		blue/gold	
P 560 Signum 1984	$35	**P 30 pen** 1966	$22
stainless steel/gold clip		black/gold (not shown)	
P 540 Signum 1984	$25	**M30 pen** 1966	$25
stainless steel, stripe-patterned		blue/gold (not shown)	
P 530 Signum 1984	$15	**M30 pen** 1966	$25
stainless steel, guilloched pattern		black/gold (not shown)	
P 510 Signum 1984	$10		
stainless steel			
Signum ca. 1980	$30		
silver-plated			
Signum ca. 1980	$60		
gold-plated (not shown)			

Souverän 760 1988 $215
gold-plated
Souverän 750 1988 $180
silver-plated (not shown)
This series was issued to honor the firm's 150th
anniversary.

P 21 Silvexa 1971 $15
black/stainless steel, cartridge
M 21 Silvexa 1971 $20
same, but piston filler
Matching ballpoint 1971 $10
Pen, completely matted ca. 1973 $22
P 15 pen 1972 $15
black/stainless steel
Pelikano pen 1960 $10
first Pelikano

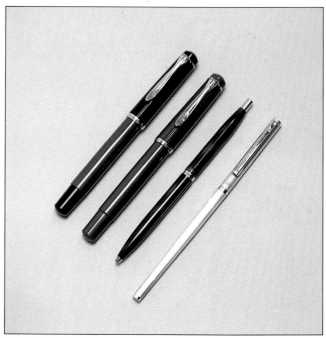

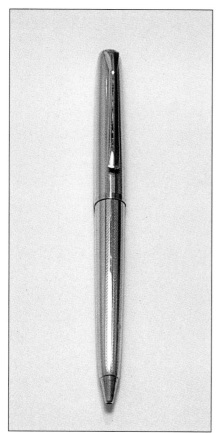

455 ballpoint 1955 $35
black
455 ballpoint 1955 $35
black/green (not shown)
455 ballpoint 1955 $35
brown/tortoiseshell (not shown)
R15 ballpoint ca. 1970 $10
red/chrome-plated
3-color 3 x 1 ca. 1970 $10
blue/stainless steel
3-color 3 x 1 ca. 1970 $10
black/stainless steel

The identifying letter before the model number
indicates the filling system. Thus M =
mechanical (piston) and P = cartridge.

585 Karat ballpoint ca. 1969 $215

M 150 1991 $45
green/black
M 100 1991 $30
green
M 100 1991 $30
brown (not shown)
Ballpoint ca. 1980 $20
blue marbled
Ballpoint ca. 1980 $35
sterling silver

All of these were export models for the Italian
market.

800 ballpoint 1994	LP $150	**Toledo 710** 1993	LP $655
green/black		sterling silver	
800 ballpoint 1994	LP $350	**Toledo 700** 1990	LP $655
green/black (not shown)		sterling silver, gold filled	
800 pencil 1994	LP $150	**Toledo 910** 1993	LP $1135
green/black (not shown)		sterling silver	
800 roller 1994	LP $195	**Toledo 900** 1993	LP $1135
green/black		sterling silver, gold filled	
800 ballpoint 1994	LP $150		
black (not shown)			
800 pen 1994	LP $350		
black (not shown)			
800 pencil 1994	LP $150		
black (not shown)			
800 roller 1994	LP $195		
black (not shown)			

Penol

Penol ca. 1935	$35
orange	
Penol No. 8 ca. 1935	$35
orange	
Penol No. 210 pencil ca. 1935	$20
orange	
Penol No. 0 ca. 1940	$22
black	
P. Ambassador Senior	$70
ca. 1940, gray striped	
Penol No. 8 ca. 1935	$70
brown marbled	
Penol No. 5 ca. 1935	$55
brown marbled	
Penol Quality Pen ca. 1950	$55
white-brown marbled	

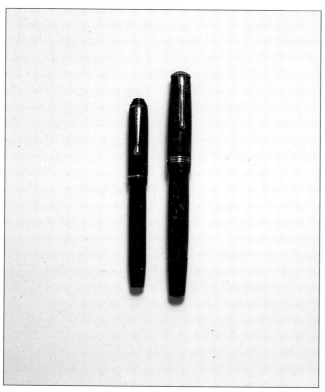

Platignum

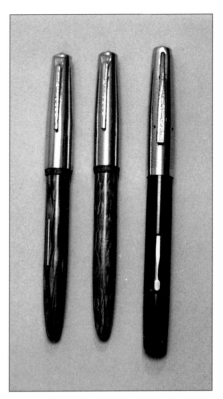

...ountain pen ca. 1950	$35
...ack	
...tylo de Luxe ca. 1940	$35
...een/black marbled	
...latignum de Luxe ca. 1930	$35
...ack and pearl	
...olden Platignum ca. 1940	$35
...een marbled	
...old Tone ca. 1950	$18
...own/gold marbled	
...old Tone ca. 1950	$15
...ay/stainless steel	
...olden Platignum ca. 1960	$10
...ue/stainless steel	
...ountain pen ca. 1960	$10
...ay	
...ountain pen ca. 1960	$10
...rquoise	
...ountain pen ca. 1960	$10
...rquoise	
...rsity ca. 1960	$10
...ck	
...verline ca. 1960	$10
...verline ca. 1960	$5
...ck/stainless steel	
...aduate Pressmatic ca. 1960	$5
...e/stainless steel	

Rotring
(1928 to date)

Tintenkuli ca. 1950, gray spotted $35
Tintenkuli ca. 1950, green striped $35
Tintenkuli ca. 1950, blue marbled $35
The Tintenkuli ballpoint was the forerunner of the cartridge
ballpoint and was produced in many color variations.

Rapidograph No. 1 1957, black, 0.3 mm $8
Rapidograph 0.3 ca. 1960, black, 0.3 mm $8
Rapidograph 0.35 ca. 1980, black, 0.35 mm   LP $25
At the beginning of the eighties, some of the sizes were
changed, with 0.3 mm becoming 0.35 mm.

Tintenkuli 117 1957, chrome-black $15
Rollkuli 211 1957, black $10
Rollkuli 1957, for the Arabian market $22
Rollkuli ca. 1960, black $10
Marked "fountain pen" for the Arabian market.

Tikk-Kuli 311 1957, black $8
Tikk-Kuli 361 1957, black/chrome $8
Kugelschreiber 1963, gold filled $15
Kugelschreiber 1980, chromed $5

Bleikuli ca. 1960, black $15
2-Farb ballpoint 371 1957, black/chrome $8
Roller 1980, stainless steel $5
Quattro Pen 1992, charcoal gray   LP $50

Fountain pen ca. 1982, green marbled $22
600 pen 1991, steel point   LP $70
600 pen 1991, black   LP $70
600 pen 1991, 14-karat gold point (not shown)   LP $135
900 pen 1992, tube filler   LP $55
900 pen 1992, steel point (not shown)   LP $70
700 pen 1993, black   LP $85
700 ballpoint 1993, black   LP $60

Sheaffer
1913 to date

Lady 1925, green with ring	$40-70
Lady ca. 1920, black with clip	$40-70
Lady pencil 1920, green	$25-35
Junior 1923, green with ring	$40-70
Junior 1923, orange with ring (not shown)	$70-110
Junior Lifetime 1923, black and pearl/clip	$60-80
5-30 1928, green with two bands	$50-75

The 5-30 series was produced as an inexpensive alternative to the Lifetime series.

Senior 1914, black guilloche, Flat Top	$150-215
Lifetime Senior 1924, black, 1 band, Flat Top	$125-175
Lifetime Senior 1928, black, 2 bands, Flat Top	$125-175
Lifetime Senior 1924, black and pearl, Flat Top	$175-250
Lifetime Senior 1924, green, 1 band, Flat Top (not shown)	$225-320
Lifetime Senior 1924, green, 2 bands, Flat Top (not shown)	$225-320

Sheaffer Lady pen ca. 1917, sterling silver	$125-175
Sheaffer pencil ca. 1917, sterling silver	$40-70
Sheaffer Lady pen ca. 1917, gold filled	$75-125
Sheaffer pencil ca. 1917, gold filled (not shown)	$30-40

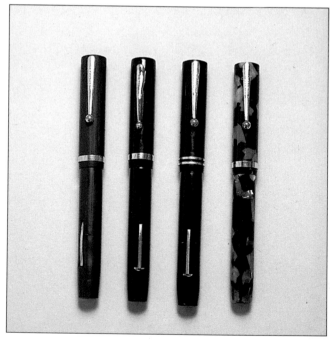

Lifetime Senior 1932 $150-225
green, streamline
Lifetime Senior 1932 $85-145
black, streamline
Lifetime Senior 1932 $75-215
black and pearl, streamline (not shown)
Lifetime Senior 1937 $100-175
gray striped
Lifetime Senior 1937 $150-225
red striped (not shown)
Lifetime Senior 1937 $100-175
brown striped (not shown)

Lady Lifetime long ca. 1932 $85-125
green
Lady Lifetime long ca. 1932 $85-125
black and pearl
All Lifetime models were marked with a white
dot. Sheaffer gave the original purchaser a
lifetime guarantee on these pens!

Combo (pen/pencil) 1930 $150-200
black
Combo (pen/pencil) 1930 $150-250
black and pearl (not shown)
Combo (pen/pencil) 1930 $175-275
green (not shown)

Junior 275 ca. 1935 $145 (set)
black/mother-of-pearl inlay

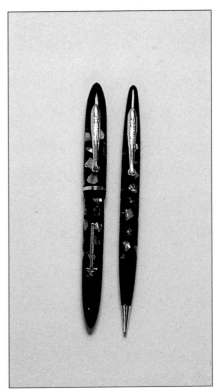

Lifetime 1936	$70	**400 pencil** 1945	$18
black		black (not shown)	
Lifetime 1000 1937	$110	**400 pencil** 1945	$20-30
gray striped, military clip		gray striped (not shown)	
Lifetime 1937	$110	**400 pencil** 1945	$20-30
brown striped		green striped	
Lifetime 1250 1937	$110	**400 pencil** 1945	$20-30
brown striped		brown striped (not shown)	
Several variations with narrow, wide and		**400 pencil** 1945	$20-30
extremely wide cap bands, as well as these in		red striped (not shown)	
different colors, were produced.			
Feather Touch 500 1945	$35	**Admiral** 1945	$55
black		black	
Feather Touch 500 1945	$55	**Admiral** 1945	$55
black, large		green	
Feather Touch 500 1945	$90	**Admiral** 1945	$70
gray striped		red striped (not shown)	
Feather Touch 500 1941	$110	**Admiral** 1945	$70
green striped, military clip		green striped (not shown)	
Feather Touch 500 1945	$90		
brown striped (not shown)			
Feather Touch 500 1945	$90		
red striped (not shown)			

Tucky pencil 1945 red	$22	**Admiral Snorkel** 1952 blue	$40-50
Tucky pencil 1945 black (not shown)	$22	**Statesman Snorkel** 1952 red	$40-50
Tucky pen 1945 red (not shown)	$55	**Statesman Snorkel** 1952 black	$40-50
Tucky pen 1945 black, narrow band	$55	**Saratoga Snorkel** 1952 gray	$40-50
Tucky pen 1945 black, broad band	$55	**Admiral Snorkel** 1952 green	$40-50
		Sentinel de Luxe Snorkel 1952, black/stainless steel	$90
Crest pen 1942 black/gold	$65-110	**Sentinel de Luxe Snorkel** 1952, gray/stainless steel	$90
Crest pencil 1942 black/gold	$35-55	**Saratoga pencil** 1952 blue (not shown)	$10-20
Crest pen 1942 gold-plated (not shown)	$125-215	**Saratoga pencil** 1952 red	$10-20
Crest pencil 1942 gold-plated (not shown)	$40-70	**Saratoga pencil** 1952 black	$10-20
Crest Opalite pen 1993 pressed cotton/gold-plated	LP $300	**Saratoga pencil** 1952 gray	$10-20
Crest Opalite ballpoint 1993 pressed cotton/gold-plated	LP $185	**Saratoga pencil** 1952 green	$10-20
Crest Opalite roller 1993 pressed cotton/gold-plated	LP $205		

This was the first time cotton was ever used as a raw material for writing instruments!

The various models can be recognized by the type of point and the white dot.

PFM Snorkel 1959 black/stainless steel cap	$145
PFM Snorkel 1959 black/gold-plated clip	$175
PFM Snorkel 1959 black/stainless steel clip (not shown) There were series with various barrel colors, with palladium silver points and gold points. PFM means Pen for Men.	$145
Touchdown Imperial 1962 black	$35
Touchdown Imperial 1962 blue	$35
Touchdown 1950 blue	$35
Pencil 1950 blue	$15
Touchdown 1950 green (not shown)	$35
Pencil 1950 green	$15
Sheaffer 3A ca. 1918 black, wave guilloche	$40-50
Sheaffer 3-25 ca. 1945 green marbled	$40-50
Sheaffer Imperial 1969 gold-plated	$35-45

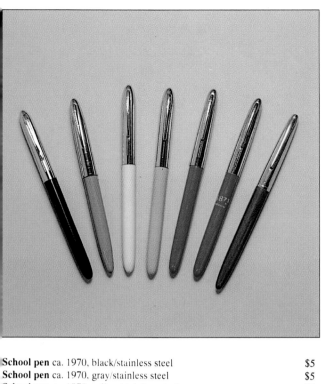

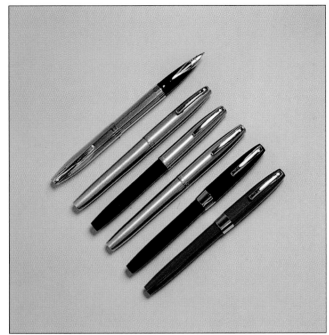

School pen ca. 1970, black/stainless steel	$5
School pen ca. 1970, gray/stainless steel	$5
School pen ca. 1970, yellow/stainless steel	$5
School pen ca. 1970, beige/stainless steel	$5
School pen ca. 1970, red/stainless steel	$5
School pen ca. 1970, red/stainless steel/gold filled clip	$8
School pen ca. 1970, gray/stainless steel/gold filled clip	$8

This series was produced in various colors.

Triumph 1960, gold-plated	$70
Triumph 1980, stainless steel, gold clip	$30
Triumph 1990, blue/stainless steel	$15
Triumph 1990, stainless steel	$22
Triumph 1990, black	$35
Triumph 1990, red	$35

Targa 1976, black, epoxy	LP $85
Targa Lady 1976, black painted	LP $235
Targa ca. 1980, silver-plated	$70
Targa Fred 1992, sterling silver	LP $725
Fred ballpoint 1992, sterling silver (not shown)	LP $620

Most Targa models wre and are issued in two versions. They are
marketed in various paint colors and metallic alloys. Painted
Targas have been made since 1979.

Nostalgia rocking blotter   LP $695
1982, sterling silver
Nostalgia fountain pen   LP $630
1980, sterling silver
Nostalgia letter opener $550
1982, sterling silver
Nostalgia ink bottle $620
1982, sterling silver
The Nostalgia pen was patterned after the
original of 1920. It was also available for a few
years in gold plated silver.

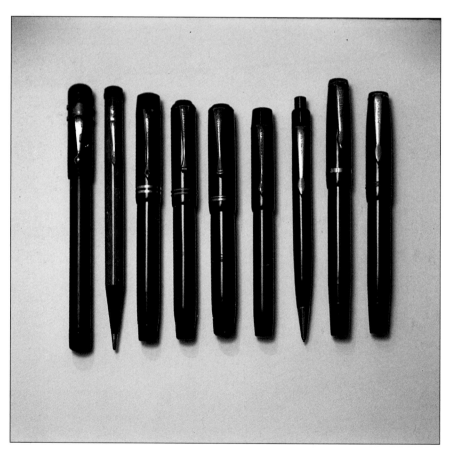

Soennecken
1868-1973

16 ca. 1910	$110
safety filler	
140 pencil ca. 1920	$55
green marbled	
1306 ca. 1940	$35
black	
1306 ca. 1940	$70
blue pearl (not shown)	
1306 ca. 1940	$70
fish pearl (not shown)	
112A 1947	$35
black	
116 1947	$45
black	
303 1935	$35
black	
Pencil ca. 1940	$15
black	
309 ca. 1940	$35
black	
412 ca. 1940	$35
black	

Swan
(1873-1957)

222 Superior 1951	$110	**444 Superior** ca. 1955	$35	**Eyedropper** 1905		$215-350
red marbled		black		gold-plated		
111 Superior 1951	$145	**School pen** 1960	$15			
dark tortoiseshell marbled		black				
Both series were made in three sizes		**100** 1960	$15			
(Lady, Superior and Extra) and five		black				
(222) or six (111) colors.		**101** 1960	$15			
		black				
		S4 1956	$22			
		black				
		S4 1956	$35			
		lilac				

Eyedropper 1500 ca. 1910	$35-55
black with shell	
Eyedropper 202 ca. 1910	$25-35
black, wave guilloche	
Eyedropper No. 2 ca. 1910	$25-35
black, Lady with ring	
Eyedropper No. 2 ca. 1910	$35-55
black, broad band	
Eyedropper No. 3 ca. 1910	$70
black, 18-karat gold band	
Eyedropper 300 ca. 1910	$25-35
black	
Eyedropper gold filled	$50-75
ca. 1910, gold filled	

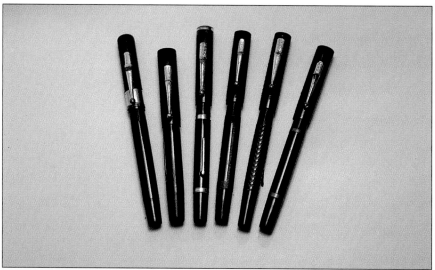

SF 2 ca. 1920	$55
black, broad band	
SF 3 ca. 1920	$35
black, without band	
230/60 ca. 1920	$70
black/Red Ripple	
SM 2/60 Minor ca. 1920	$35
black, stripe guilloche	
42 Posting ca. 1920	$35
black, wave guilloche	
Self Filler ca. 1920	$35
black, two brown bands	

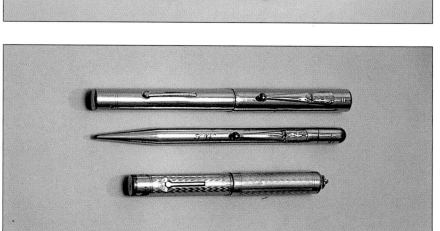

Swan gold filled ca. 1920	$75-150
Pencil gold filled ca. 1920	$35
Swan Lady ca. 1920	$50-70
with ring	

Swan ca. 1920 $110-135
sterling silver
42 ca. 1922 $70
Red Ripple
1 S.F. ca. 1922 $55
Red Ripple
1 S.F. ca. 1922 $30
black (not shown)
2 S.F. ca. 1922 $35
black (not shown)
272/52 ca. 1925 $55
Lady, ring, blue marbled

Eternal 42 1925 $100-150
Red Ripple
Eternal 42 1925 $70
black (not shown)
Eternal 44 1925 $175-215
Red Ripple (not shown)

Eternal 44 1925 $110
black (not shown)
Eternal 46 1925 $285
Red Ripple (not shown)
Eternal 46 1925 $145
black (not shown)

Swan Lady ca. 1920 $178
9-karat gold, ring
Fyne Point pencil ca. 1920 $110
9-karat gold, wave guilloche
Swan ca. 1920 $285
15-karat stripe guilloche

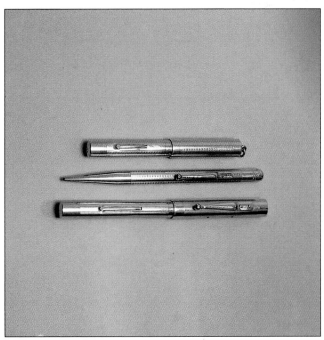

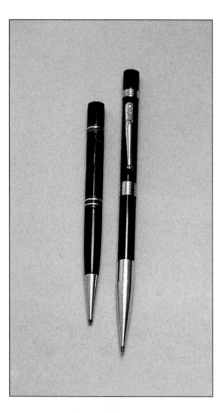

Fyne Point pencil ca. 1930 black, green-gold	$42
Fyne Point pencil ca. 1930 black, gold filled bands	$55
Kiwi ca. 1940 black	$30
Swallow ca. 1940 black	$30
Jackdaw ca. 1930 Red Ripple	$55
Jackdaw ca. 1940 gray-brown marbled	$70

Pens with bird names, such as
Blackbird, Kiwi, Swallow and Jackdaw
belong to the Mabie Todd Group.

Blackbird Eyedropper ca. 1925, black	$30
Blackbird 2/60 ca. 1935 black, crossline guilloche	$30
Blackbird 2/60 ca. 1935 black, crossline guilloche	$30
Blackbird ca. 1935 black, two gold filled bands	$55
Blackbird ca. 1935 black with clip	$35
Blackbird 5242 ca. 1940 blue marbled	$55
Blackbird 2 G 2 ca. 1940 green marbled	$55
Blackbird ca. 1950 blue marbled	$35
Blackbird ca. 1950 green, gold filled cap	$35

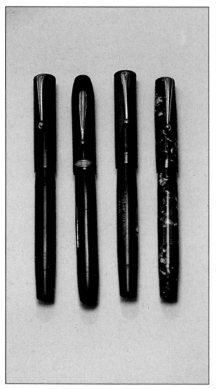

Visofil VT 340/76 ca. 1935 $145
green marbled

Leverless ca. 1935 $75-175
gold-plated

Leverless L 205/60 ca. 1935 $35
black

Leverless L 212/66 ca. 1935 $90
green-black marbled

Leverless ca. 1940 $35
black

Leverless 312/60 ca. 1940 $55
black

Leverless 1060 ca. 1940 $70
black

Leverless 42/60 ca. 1945 $35
black

Leverless ca. 1945 $55
black

Leverless 4 point 1950 $70
black

Leverless 4 point 1950 $70
other solid colors (not shown)

Leverless 5 point 1950 $110
Solid colors (not shown)

Leverless 6 point 1950 $145
green

Leverless 6 point 1950 $145
black

Leverless 6 point 1950 $145
solid colors (not shown)

SM 2/57 ca. 1935 $70
blue-brown marbled

SM 100/63 ca. 1940 $55
black/brown marbled

Swan ca. 1940 $55
gray marbled

Swan ca. 1940 $55
green marbled

Swan ca. 1940 $70
blue marbled

Swan ca. 1940 $70
gray marbled

Swan ca. 1940 $70
blue marbled

SM 205/63 ca. 1940 $70
green-blue-black

SM 100/62 ca. 1940 $70
green-red marbled

9241 ca. 1940 $55
green marbled

SM 100/84 ca. 1940 $70
green marbled

SM 100/85 ca. 1940 $70
brown marbled

SM 100/86 ca. 1940 $70
gray marbled

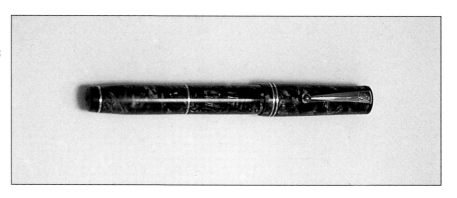

Swan ca. 1940		$35
blue		
Swan ca. 1940		$30
black		
Swan ca. 1940		$30
black		
Swan ca. 1945		$30
black		
SM 205/60 ca. 1945		$30
black, wave guilloche		
62/20 ca. 1945		$30
black		
3120 ca. 1950		$30

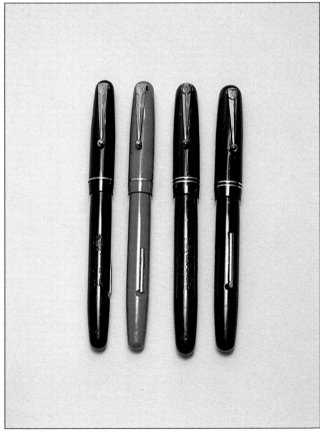

dark blue, one band	
3130 ca. 1950	$30
gray, one band	
3140 ca. 1950	$30
dark green, one band (not shown)	
3150 ca. 1950	$30
dark brown, one band (not shown)	
3160 ca. 1950	$30
black, one band (not shown)	
3220 ca. 1950	$35
dark blue, two bands (not shown)	
3230 ca. 1950	$35
gray, two bands (not shown)	
3240 ca. 1950	$35
dark green, two bands	
3250 ca. 1950	$35
dark brown, two bands	
3260 ca. 1950	$35
black, two bands (not shown)	

Wahl-Eversharp
(1912-1957)

Gold filled pencil, lady's size	$15-25
ca. 1920, smooth, round, with ring	
Gold filled pencil, lady's size	$15-25
ca. 1920, V-pattern, with ring	
Gold filled pencil, lady's size	$25-35
ca. 1920, smooth, octagonal, with clip	
Gold filled pencil, lady's size	$15-25
ca. 1920, with ring and box	
Gold filled pencil, lady's size	$20-30
ca. 1920, stripes, with clip	
Gold filled pencil, man's size	$45-55
ca. 1920, stripes	
Gold filled pencil, man's size	$45-55
ca. 1920, V pattern	
Gold filled pencil, man's size	$45-55
ca. 1920, smooth	
14-karat gold pencil	$175
ca. 1920, smooth	

(All pencils made by Wahl-Eversharp.)
In the twenties, many different designs were
produced; most of them have the same values.

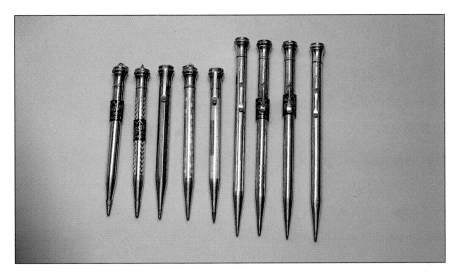

Eversharp pencil 1917	$15-20
gold-plated, smooth, with ring	
Wahl-Eversharp pencil 1919	$15-20
gold-plated, with ring and box	
Wahl-Eversharp pencil ca. 1930	$35
lilac/black, with clip	
Eversharp pencil 1926	$25-35
Red Ripple, with ring	
Eversharp pencil 1917	$20-30
silver-plated, smooth, with ring	
Wahl-Eversharp pencil 1925	$25-35
orange, with ring	
Wahl-Eversharp pencil 1925	$35
blue, with ring	

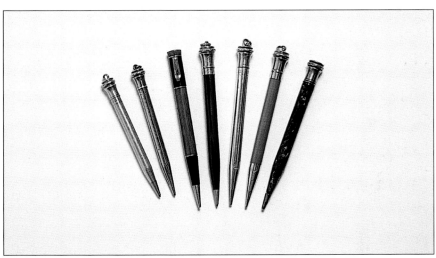

Wahl Pen 1922	$70
gold-plated, with ring and box	
Wahl Pen 1922	$90
gold-plated, lined, with clip	
Wahl Pen 1925	$90
gold-plated, V pattern, with clip	
Wahl-Eversharp Pen	$110
ca. 1925, gold-plated, black enamel	
Wahl Pen ca. 1925	$70
Art Deco pattern, clip	
Wahl Pen ca. 1925	$70
Art Deco pattern, clip	
Wahl Pen ca. 1925	$50-70
Art Deco pattern, ring	

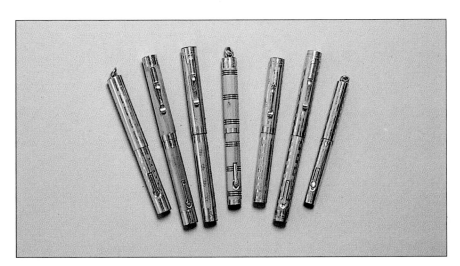

Wahl pen 1933	$55
red marbled	
Wahl pencil 1933	$18
red marbled	
Wahl pen 1933	$55
blue marbled	
Wahl pencil 1933	$18
blue marbled (not shown)	
Wahl pen 1933	$55
green marbled	
Wahl pencil 1933	$18
green marbled	

Eversharp Doric 1935	$155
green marbled	
Eversharp Doric 1935	$180
blue marbled (not shown)	
Eversharp Doric 1935	$145
black	
Eversharp Doric pencil 1935	$50-70
black	
Eversharp Doric 1935	$155
gold/green marbled	
Eversharp Doric 1935	$155
silver marbled (not shown)	

Pencils matching the series of pens are
worth 1/3 the value of the fountain pen.

Wahl-Ev. Gold Seal pen	$90
ca. 1930, black	
Wahl-Ev. Gold Seal pencil	$35
ca. 1930, black	
Wahl-Eversharp pen	$70
ca. 1929, black and pearl	
Wahl-Ev. Gold Seal pen	$110-200
1927, black and pearl	
Wahl-Ev. Gold Seal pen	$110-200
1927, green/gold (not shown)	
Wahl-Ev. Gold Seal pen	$70-145
1927, black	
Wahl-Ev. Gold Seal pen	$110-200
1927, Red Ripple (not shown)	
Wahl-Ev. Gold Seal pen	$145-225
1927, blue marbled (not shown)	

Wahl-Eversharp pen	$90	**Eversharp No. 4 pencil**	$8
ca. 1935, black		1925, black	
Wahl-Eversharp pencil	$35	**Eversharp gold filled pencil**	$35-45
ca. 1935, black		ca. 1922, zigzag lines	
Wahl-Eversharp pen	$125	**Ever. Repeater pencil**	$35-45
ca. 1935, green marbled		1936, gold filled with black panels	
Wahl-Eversharp pencil	$55	**Eversharp Repeater pencil**	$35-45
ca. 1935, green marbled (not shown)		1936, gold filled cap, colored	
		barrel (not shown)	
Wahl-Eversharp Junior	$55	**Eversharp Repeater pencil**	$35-45
ca. 1940, gray marbled		1936, rhodium cap/green (not shown)	
Wahl-Ever. Pacemaker	$110	**Eversharp Repeater pencil**	$35-45
1938, green marbled		1936, rhodium cap/red (not shown)	
Both versions were made in numerous colors.		**Eversharp pencil** ca. 1950	$8
		blue	
		This list of pencils offers only a small	
		selection of the entire assortment.	

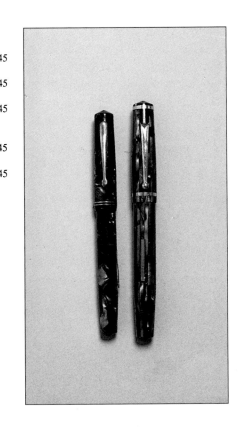

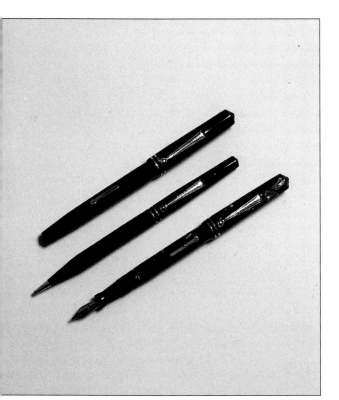

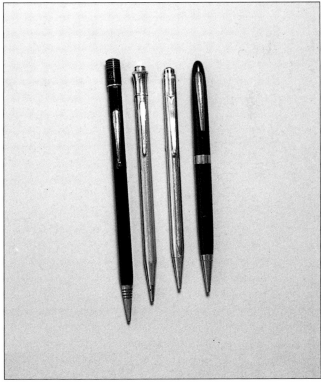

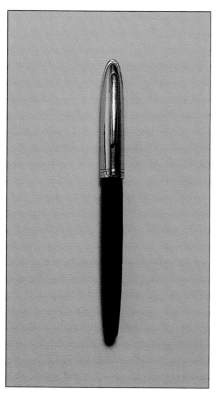

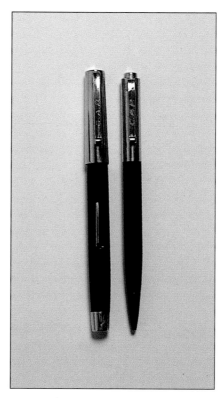

Eversharp Skyline pen $90
1941, brown, gold-plated cap
Eversharp Skyline pencil $35
1941, red, gold-plated cap
Eversharp Skyline pencil $30
1941, red
Eversharp Skyline pencil $30
1941, gray and other solid colors
Eversharp Skyline pen $75-125
1941, blue stripes (not shown)
Eversharp Skyline pen $75-125
1941, green striped (not shown)
Eversharp Skyline pen $90
1941, solid-color barrel, striped cap
(not shown)
Eversharp Skyline pen $55
1941, solid-color barrel and cap (not
shown)
Eversharp Skyline pencil $150
1941, 14-karat gold
Eversharp Skyline pen $360
1941, 14-karat gold

Ever. 5th Avenue pencil $110
1944, 14-karat gold/maroon
Ever. 5th Avenue pen $180
1944, 14-karat gold/maroon
There are series with blue, green, gray
and black lower parts.

Eversharp Symphony 1950 $30
green/chrome-plated
Eversharp Symphony 1950 $30
black/chrome-plated (not shown)

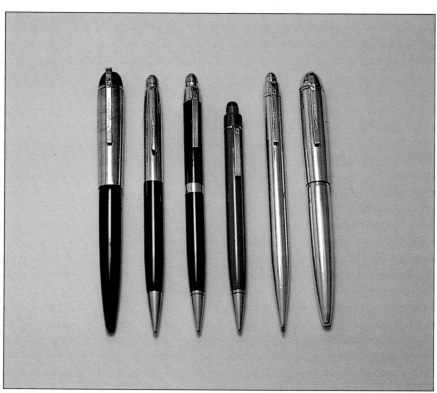

Waterman (1884 to date)

Eyedropper 2 ca. 1900	$55	552 1/2 LEC ca. 1915	$360
black		9-karat gold	
Eyedropper 12 1910	$55	0552 1/2 Sheraton ca. 1915	$145
black, stick-on cap		gold-plated	
Eyedropper 14 1910	$70	552 ca. 1915	$530
black, stick-on cap (not shown)		9-karat gold	
Eyedropper 15 1910	$110	0552 Gothic ca. 1915	$285
black, stick-on cap (not shown)		gold-plated, without clip	
Eyedropper 18 1910	$350-500	452 Gothic Sterling ca. 1915	$285
black, stick-on cap (not shown)		with clip	
Eyedropper 20 1910	$900-1100	412 1/2 V.S. Baby 1920	$180
black, stick-on cap (not shown)		safety pen in sterling silver	
Eyedropper 74 ca. 1910	$145	452 1/2 V Gothic 1920	$145
black, screw-on cap		lever filler in sterling silver	
Eyedropper 75 ca. 1910	$145	452 1/2 V Sheraton 1920	$145
black, screw-on cap		lever filler in sterling silver	
		0552 1/2 V Sheraton 1920	$160
		lever filler, gold-plated	
		Filigree pencil 1920	$35-55
		gold-plated	

All models were available with various point sizes, gold-plating, with silver decorations and in solid gold.

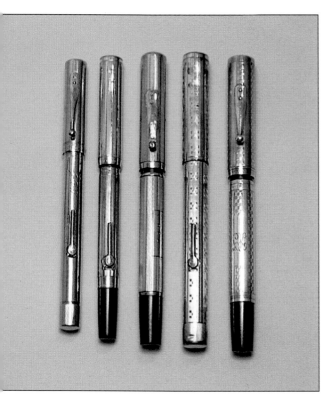

52 1/2 V 1923	$50-70
red marbled (not shown)	
Red Ripple pencil 1923	$35-45
red/brown marbled	
52 Red Ripple 1923	$125
red/brown marbled	
54 Red Ripple 1923	$135
red/brown marbled (not shown)	
55 Red Ripple 1923	$175
red/brown marbled, 9-karat gold	
56 Red Ripple 1923	$225
red/brown marbled	
58 Red Ripple 1923	$750-80◖
red/brown marbled (not shown)	
7 Red Ripple 1923	$285
same, with brown band	
Red Ripple pencil 1923	$145
with 9-karat gold decorations	

Model 7 existed in various color codes.
These referred to the point width.

52 Red Ripple 1923	$125
without cap band	
Red Ripple pencil 1923	$35-45
without cap band	

92 1/2 1925	$70
black	
52 1/2 V 1925	$55
black	
52 1/2 1925	$90
black	
0652 1925	$110
black, two gold filled bands	
52 1925	$70
black	
54 1925	$70
black	
54 1925	$110
black (not shown)	
55 1925	$145
black	
56 1925	$175
black	
58 1925	$300-45◖
black (not shown)	

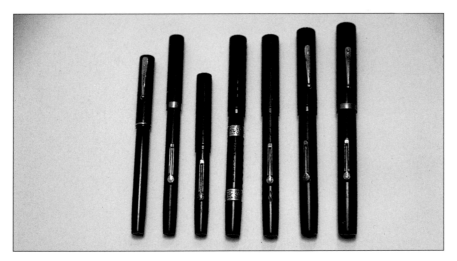

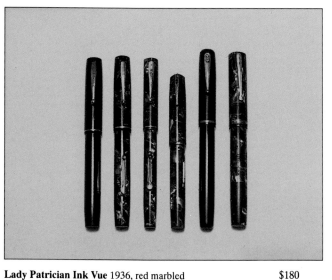

Lady Patrician Ink Vue 1936, red marbled	$180
Lady Patrician Ink Vue 1936, gray marbled	$180
(not shown)	
Lady Patrician Ink Vue 1936, black (not shown)	$180
Lady Patrician 1930, onyx	$75-145
Lady Patrician 1930, black (not shown)	$75-145
Lady Patrician 1930, green (not shown)	$80-160
Lady Patrician 1930, moss agate (green/brown)	$80-160
(not shown)	
Lady Patrician 1930, blue/gold (not shown)	$80-160
Patrician 1929, onyx	$530-600
Patrician 1929, black (not shown)	$530-600
Patrician 1929, green (not shown)	$650-800
Patrician 1929, moss agate (green/brown)	$650-800
Patrician 1929, blue/gold (not shown)	$710-900
Lady Patrician pencil 1930, any version	$35-55
Patrician pencil 1929, any version (not shown)	$100-145
Waterman 7 1930, black	$145
Waterman 5 1930, black (not shown)	$90
32 1933, black	$42
32 1933, green marbled	$90
32 1/2 1931, green marbled	$70
3 V 1933, black (not shown)	$42
3 V 1933, gray/brown marbled	$55
92 1932, black	$42
92 1932, gray marbled (not shown)	$70
92 1932, green/gold marbled (not shown)	$70
92 1932, red/gold marbled (not shown)	$70
94 1932, black (not shown)	$55
94 1932, gray/red marbled	$90
94 1932, green/gold marbled (not shown)	$90
94 1932, red/gold marbled (not shown)	$90

Junior ca. 1935	$30-42
black	
Junior ca. 1935	$50-70
copper marbled	
Junior ca. 1935	$50-70
blue marbled	
Ink Vue 1935	$70-110
black	
Ink Vue 1935	$85-145
silver marbled (not shown)	
Ink Vue 1935	$85-145
red marbled (not shown)	
Ink Vue 1935	$85-145
green marbled (not shown)	
Pencil 1932	$35-55
gray marbled	
Pencil ca. 1945	$30-42
red marbled	
Pencil ca. 1960	$20-22
black	
W 3 ca. 1950, green	$30
W 3 ca. 1950, black, other solid colors (not shown)	$30
W 3 ca. 1950, blue striped	$70
W 3 ca. 1950, green striped and others, marbled (not shown)	$55
W 5 ca. 1950, black	$35
W 5 ca. 1950, other solid colors (not shown)	$35
W 5 ca. 1950, green striped	$70
W 5 ca. 1950, blue striped and others, marbled (not shown)	$90

503 (red dot) ca. 1950	$55
bookkeeping fountain pen	
503 (white dot) ca. 1950	$55
stenographic fountain pen	
503 ca. 1950	$30
black	
503 ca. 1950	$30
other colors (not shown)	
512 ca. 1950	$42
gray marbled	
512 ca. 1950	$42
other colors, marbled (not shown)	
513 ca. 1950	$55
blue marbled	
513 ca. 1950	$42
black	
513 ca. 1950	$55
gray marbled	
513 ca. 1950	$55
other colors, marbled (not shown)	
515 ca. 1950	$42
red	
Pencil matching 515 ca. 1950	$18
red	
515 ca. 1950	$55
dark brown	
515 ca. 1950	$42
blue	
515 ca. 1950	$42
other colors (not shown)	

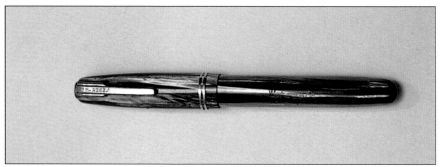

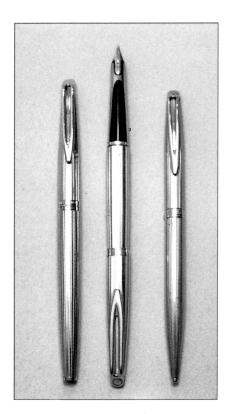

CF ballpoint 1953	$45-65
silver-plated	
CF ballpoint 1953	$40-50
silver-plated (not shown)	
CF pen 1953	$110
sterling silver (not shown)	
CF ballpoint 1953	$45-65
sterling silver (not shown)	
CF pen 1953	$110
gold-plated	
CF ballpoint 1953	$45-65
gold-plated (not shown)	
CF pen 1953	$425
18-karat gold (not shown)	
CF ballpoint 1953	$285-325
18-karat gold	
Hundred Year Pen	$145-400
1939, black	
Watermans ca. 1940	$90
black	
Crusader 1948	$35-42
Lady, blue/gold filled	
Taperite 1948	$55
black/gold filled	
Taperite ca. 1960	$18
red/stainless steel	

The 100 Year Pen was made in various colors in both men's and ladies' versions.

Waterman 1970	$22
Lady, stainless steel	
Waterman 1970	$30
stainless steel	
Waterman 1970	$30
lilac	
Waterman 1970	$30
black/gold	
Waterman 1970	$30
brown (not shown)	

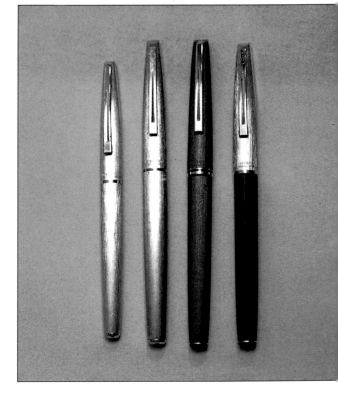

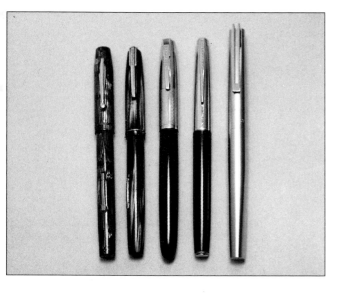

Skywriter ca. 1940 gray striped	$45-50	**Man 200 Caviar** 1990 white marbled	LP $320
Waterman's ca. 1950 brown marbled	$35-55	**Man 200 Rhapsody** ca. 1990, painted wood structure	LP $320
Waterman's 1950 black/gold	$30-42	**Man 100 Arlequin** 1991 black with markings	LP $400
Waterman's ca. 1970 black/stainless steel	$15-22	**Man 100 Opera** ca. 1989 black with waves	LP $490
Waterman Man 1967 stainless steel	$110	**Man 100 Sterling pen** ca. 1988, sterling silver	LP $850
Waterman Man 1967 black (not shown)	$110	**Man 100 Sterling ballpoint** ca. 1988, sterling silver	LP $460
Man 200 blue/Rhapsody 1990, blue marbled	LP $320	**Man 100 Patrician pen** 1992, green marbled	LP $490

LP $265
LP $490
LP $265
LP $490
LP $265
LP $850
LP $440

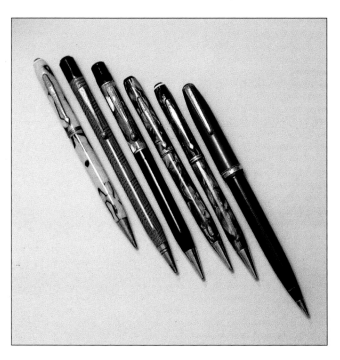

Wearever

Pencil ca. 1930 black and pearl	$22
Pencil ca. 1930 red with markings	$22
Pencil ca. 1940 black/green	$22

Pencil ca. 1940 green marbled	$18
Pencil ca. 1940 red marbled	$18
Combi pen/pencil ca. 1940 red	$35
Pen ca. 1935 black and pearl	$55
Pen ca. 1935 black and pearl	$35
Pen ca. 1940 white-black striped	$35
Pen ca. 1940 green/brown marbled	$35
De Luxe 100 ca. 1950 red/black marbled	$35
De Luxe 100 ca. 1950 green marbled	$35
De Luxe ca. 1950 gray striped	$35
Pen ca. 1950 red marbled	$22
Pen ca. 1960 black	$15
Pen ca. 1960 blue/stainless steel	$15
Pen ca. 1960 green/gold filled	$15
Ballpoint ca. 1960 green/gold filled	$8-12

Various Brands

Ingersoll no. 1 1/2 1925 $35-45
red
Ingersoll no. 1 1/2 1925 $35-45
brown

Ingersoll no. 1323 pencil 1925 $20-35
gold-plated
Ingersoll no. 1329 1925 $20-35
gold-plated
Ingersoll no. 320 B 1925 $10-15
silver-plated
Ingersoll Dollar Pen 1925 $25-35
metal case

Eagle ca. 1930 $125-175
green marbled
Eagle ca. 1930 $125-175
black and pearl

Eagle ca. 1940 $30
blue/gray marbled
Eagle ca. 1940 $30
pink/red marbled

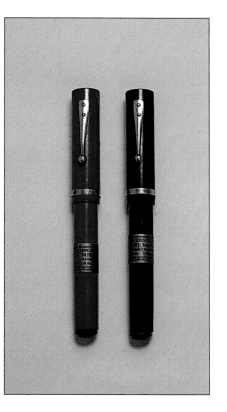

Welsh Combo ca. 1935	$70
red marbled	
No name Combo ca. 1935	$70
green marbled	
Astoria Combo ca. 1950	$30
black	
Big Ben ca. 1940	$30
black	
Caesar ca. 1950	$35
gray striped	
Caesar ca. 1950	$55
blue marbled	
True Point ca. 1950	$30
red	
True Point ca. 1950	$35
black	
Osmirold ca. 1960	$15
red	
Rex 110 ca. 1960	$18
gray	
No name ca. 1925	$55
Lady's fountain pen, gold filled	
Broadway ca. 1930	$90
gold filled, stripe guilloche	
B. B. ca. 1960	$30
gold filled/green	
No name ca. 1960	$30
gold filled	
Penman ca. 1960	$30
aluminum	

Camel ca. 1935 $55-75
black
Summit ca. 1940 $22
gray
Moore 72a ca. 1940 $25-40
black
Ink-D-Cator ca. 1940 $18
black
No name ca. 1940 $55
black, wave guilloche
No name ca. 1940 $30
black, smooth

Wyvern No. 60 ca. 1945 $55
gray speckled
Wyvern No. 60 ca. 1945 $55
brown speckled
Wyvern Perfect ca. 1945 $30
green marbled
Wyvern ca. 1945 $42
red marbled
Wyvern 404 ca. 1950 $22
dark brown
Summit ca. 1945 $30
green marbled

Conklin Endura ca. 1940 $55-75
black
Croxley ca. 1950 $18
black
Croxley ca. 1950 $42
brown marbled
Hoover 336 ca. 1940 $70
brown marbled
Hoover 873 ca. 1950 $35
gray marbled
Acca 84 ca. 1950 $35
red marbled
Miller 697 ca. 1940 $70
brown marbled
Cleveland ca. 1940 $70
brown marbled
Cleveland ca. 1940 $55
brown marbled
National Security ca. 1940 $55
blue/gold marbled
Welsh ca. 1950 $30
brown marbled
Nova ca. 1950 $35
gray marbled
Gold Medal ca. 1950 $30
red striped
Chatsworth ca. 1950 $30
gray marbled

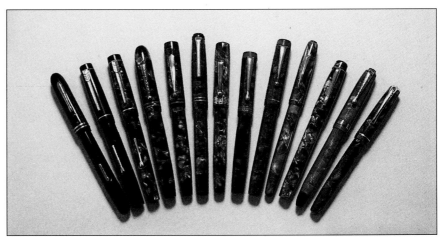

Lewis ca. 1925 Red Ripple	$75-110
No name ca. 1925 Red Ripple	$50-90
Townsend ca. 1925 Red Ripple	$100-145
Lincoln ca. 1925 Red Ripple	$125-175
No name ca. 1930 Lady's green pen	$35
Cameron ca. 1930 black checkerboard pattern	$70
No name ca. 1930 black wave guilloche	$22
No name ca. 1930 black, smooth	$35
Eclipse ca. 1930 black	$35
Kingswood ca. 1935 green marbled	$35
No name ca. 1930 black, two bands	$55
Chilton 1935 red with initials	$70
Accurate ca. 1930, orange	$50-75
Pyralin ca. 1930, green striped	$50-75
Ambassador ca. 1930, green marbled	$50-75
No name ca. 1940, black, skyline shape	$20-30
No name ca. 1935, black	$20-30
Poker ca. 1930, green marbled	$20-30

No name ca. 1930 $35
glass point and body
Ambassador ca. 1930 $70
green marbled
Lincoln ca. 1930 $50-75
orange
Boston ca. 1950 $40-60
red marbled

Combo no name ca. 1940 $22
beige
Wyvern Combina No. 1 ca. 1940 $70
black
Combi no name ca. 1930 $40-60
green
Combi Packard ca. 1940 $40-60
black/gold

Mentmore ca. 1950 $18
black
Mentmore ca. 1950 $18
green marbled
Mentmore ca. 1950 $35
brown marbled
Mentmore ca. 1950 $35
blue marbled

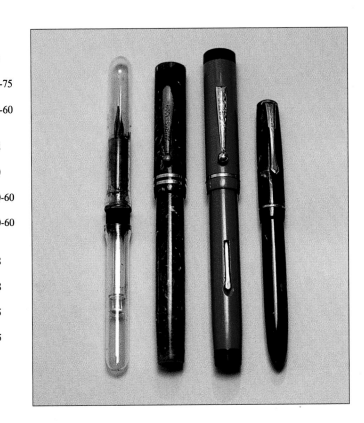

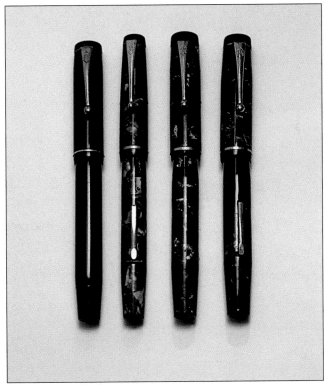

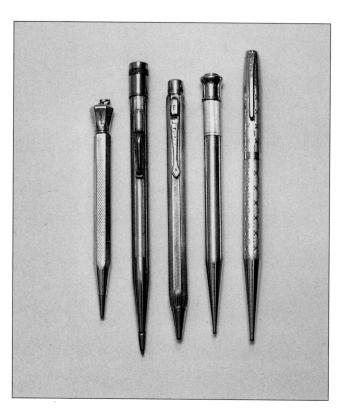

Life Long ca. 1930	$22
sterling silver	
Brevete ca. 1940	$18
silver-plated	
Stator ca. 1930	$30
900 silver	
Mordan ca. 1930	$30-50
gold-plated	
Yard-o-Led ca. 1940	$55
gold-plated, wave guilloche	
Pencil/Ruler ca. 1950	$70
sterling silver, extendable	
Napi 3-color lead ca. 1940	$30
blue	
Big Ben ca. 1950	$30
green speckled	
Big Ben ca. 1950	$42
green speckled	
No name ca. 1960	$18
gray/red marbled	
Presspoint ca. 1940	$30
green marbled	
Bittwell ca. 1940	$30
green marbled	
No name ca. 1940	$30
brown/white/blue marbled	

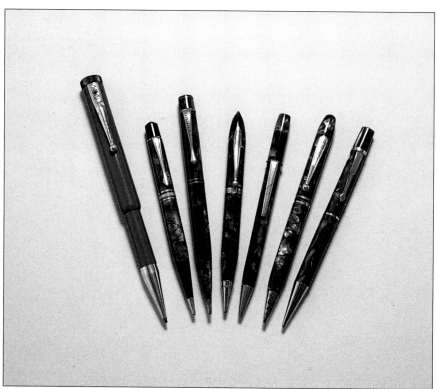

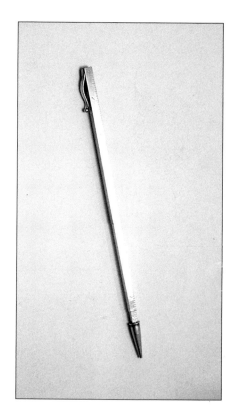

uxor 59 ca. 1940 $55
speckled
ca. 1940 $55
rbled
101c ca. 1945 $35
rbled
366 ca. 1945 $35
, gold filled cap
r ca. 1960 $8
/stainless steel
r Steno ca. 1965 $5
k/stainless steel

ador Express 810 ca. 1945 $22
ck
atador Express 814 ca. 1945 $30
lack
Matador Click 002 ca. 1950 $22
black

Brause ca. 1940, black $30
Brause ca. 1950, black $22
Brause 3032 transparent ca. 1960, two-stage tank $55
Brause 3033 ca. 1950, black $22
Brause 3050 ca. 1960, black $15
Brause 3033 ca. 1960, two-stage tank, black $30
Brause 3000 ca. 1960, black $22

MORE ON *Pens*

THE ILLUSTRATED GUIDE TO
ANTIQUE WRITING INSTRUMENTS

STUART SCHNEIDER & GEORGE FISCHLER

This is the kind of guide collectors need for quick and easy reference. Both handy and beautiful, it shows over 500 pens and pencils in nearly full-size color photos and provides short histories of the 19 main companies. Concise, helpful information with each photo includes a guide to the price of each.

Size: 6" x 9"
556 color photos
160 pp
ISBN: 0-7643-0251-5
soft cover
$19.95

THE BOOK OF
FOUNTAIN PENS
AND PENCILS

STUART SCHNEIDER & GEORGE FISCHLER

Over 700 pens and pencils, pictured in full color, with valuable information from two of the world's leading authorities. The book also deals with pen company advertising, pen repair, decoration, and valuation. Hundreds of manufacturers are represented in full-color, life-sized photos.

9" x 12"
Value guide
276 pp.
Over 700 pens illustrated in full color
ISBN: 0-88740-394-8
hard cover
$79.95

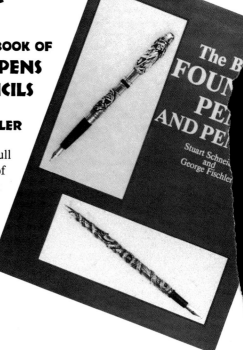

OLLECTING WRITING INSTRUMENTS

ETMAR GEYER

om the flint tool to the stylus, from the quill pen to the fountain
n and felt-tip marker, this book invites one to develop or deepen
e's love for beautiful old writing instruments. Contains 100s of
ntemporary engravings, illustrations, advertisements, photos,
d catalog and brochure excerpts.

ze: 9" x 12"
ce guide
6 pp.
BN: 0-88740-272-0
rd cover
).95

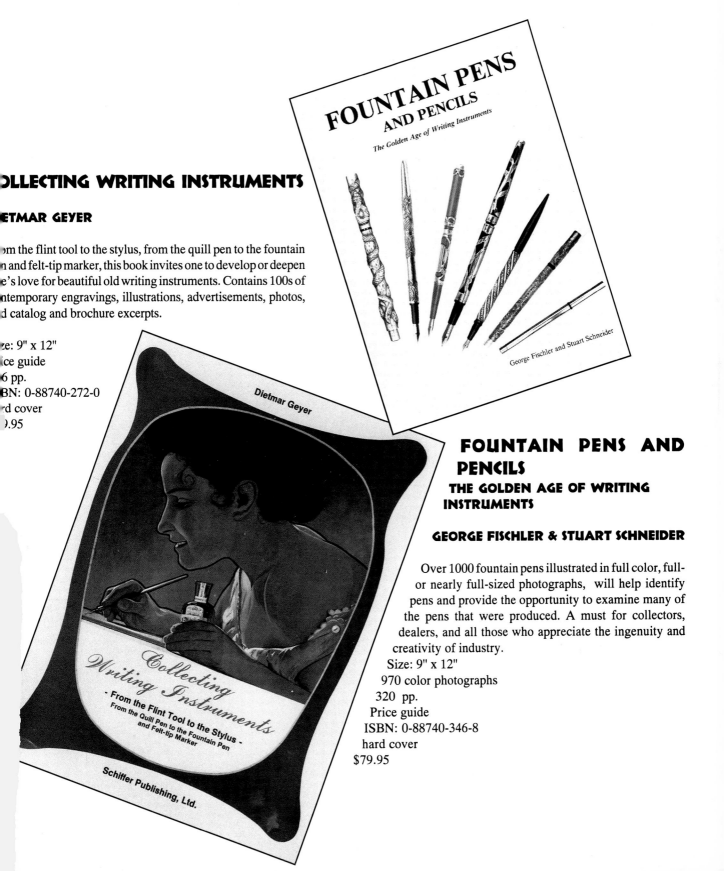

FOUNTAIN PENS AND PENCILS
THE GOLDEN AGE OF WRITING INSTRUMENTS

GEORGE FISCHLER & STUART SCHNEIDER

Over 1000 fountain pens illustrated in full color, full-
or nearly full-sized photographs, will help identify
pens and provide the opportunity to examine many of
the pens that were produced. A must for collectors,
dealers, and all those who appreciate the ingenuity and
creativity of industry.

Size: 9" x 12"
970 color photographs
320 pp.
Price guide
ISBN: 0-88740-346-8
hard cover
$79.95

AND OTHER *Timele*

AUTOMATIC WRISTWATCHES FROM SWITZERLAND
WATCHES THAT WIND THEMSELVES

HEINZ HAMPEL

Here 200 watches are shown, each with three photos to show the dial, and the complete and partly disassembled movement. The book introduces all the Swiss manufacturers and provides an historical overview of the development of automatic watches from 1926 to 1978. Information on the functioning mechanism and construction of each design is offered along with the data needed to locate the watches chronologically.

Price Guide
Size: 9" x 12"
500+ photos
352pp.
ISBN: 0-88740-609-2
Hard cover
 $79.95

BREITLING TIMEPIECES
1884 TO THE PRESENT

BENNO RICHTER

This book shows the whole spectrum of the firm's products since its founding in 1884, and gives the reader an informed insight into more than 100 years of the firm's history, including its most famous watch, then Navitimer. Many photos, old catalogs and advertising material support the informative text. With the help of reference numbers, the collector can also locate individual watches chronologically.

Size: 8 1/2" X 11"
Hard cover
176pp.
537 timepieces 50 color plate
272 halftones
ISBN: 0-88740-864-8
 $49.95

EASURES

AMERICAN WRISTWATCHES
FIVE DECADES OF STYLE AND DESIGN

EDWARD FABER & STEWART UNGER
WITH ETTAGALE BLAUER

The authors have traced the history of the American wristwatch. Original research brings life to some of the persons who influenced its development. Design periods are defined and the watches they engendered are amply illustrated.

Size: 9" x 12"
Price guide
272 pp.
698 color photographs
12 b/w photographs
ISBN: 0-7643-0171-3
hard cover
$79.95

RUSSIAN WRISTWATCHES
POCKET WATCHES,
STOP WATCHES, ONBOARD
CLOCK & CHRONOMETERS

JURI LEVENBERG

This new book will satisfy even the most avid enthusiast, with photographs of over 500 watches manufactured in Russia and the USSR during the second half of this century, and explanations of their styles, workings, and manufacturers. Poljot, Wostok, and Slava wristwatches are covered, along with a sampling of pocket watches, deck watches, and marine chronometers. Watch faces commemorate all the great moments of Russian and Soviet history.

Size 7" X 10"
Price Guide
96pp.
505 timepieces 19 color photos
ISBN: 0-88740-873-7
soft cover
$19.95

FROM *Schiffe*

TIME IN GOLD
WRISTWATCHES

GERALD VIOLA & GISBERT L. BRUNNER

The history of the 18 leading luxury wristwatch companies of Switzerland are presented together for the first time. Beautifully illustrated with color photos here are the most important and elegant watches of Audemars Piguet, Baume & Mercier, Blancpain, Breguet Cartier, Chopad, Corum, Ebel, Gerald Genta, Gerard Perregaux, IWC, Jaeger-LeCoultre, Patek Philippe, Piaget Rolex, Ulysse Nardin, Vacheron Constantin, and Technische Kapitel.

Size: 9" x 12"
256 pp.
450 illustrations, most in full color
ISBN: 0-88740-137-6
hard cover
$79.95

WRISTWATCHES
HISTORY OF A CENTURY'S DEVELOPMENT

HELMUT KAHLERT, RICHARD MUHË, GISBERT L. BRUNNER

The fascinating world of wristwatches shown through illustrated examples. Wristwatches from around the world, their makers, technological changes, construction, and automatic features are discussed. Price guide by noted authority Gordon Converse.

Size: 9" x 12"
Over 1500 watches
410 pp.
126 pages in color
1,672 b/w photographs
196 drawings and illustrations
ISBN: 0-88740-070-1
hard cover
$79.95